SEX ON THE BRAIN

Explore the History and Psychology of Human Sexuality and the Emotional, Physical and Spiritual Connection Acquired by Developing Sexual Intelligence

Belle Rogers

Table of Contents

Introduction

We need to talk.

Many a conversation that starts with these four words never ends well. This conversation, however, is different. We need to talk about sex!

Sex is a subject that most people go through with assumptions. Assumptions can only get you so far. There comes a point in time when you realize that there is so much you probably didn't know about sex. There is a lot about sex that revolves around our lives that we might not be aware of. We believe we are perfect just the way we are, but the lifestyle we lead tells a different story altogether.

The human body is subject to many changes over the course of our lives. As our bodies change, so does sex and our ability to enjoy it. Our perceptions about sex will also change according to the life we live. For example, during our younger years, most of us are inclined towards participating in sex for the adrenaline rush. Our hormones act in such a way that we feel the urge and need to act on it as soon as possible.

However, things change as we grow older. Experiences teach us different things about ourselves and our sex lives that influence the way we see sex. It is unfortunate that some people forego sex altogether, because they feel they are unable to perform as they should, or they cannot enjoy sex the way they used to. All is not lost, however, as we will learn in this book.

There are many insecurities we harbor about sex that prevent us from enjoying the best of it. If we can overcome these insecurities, we have a better chance of living a happy and

5

satisfactory life. You should also understand the phase of life you are going through, to help you understand your sexual tendencies. For example, in our younger years, most of our sexual desires are driven by urgency and instinct. We get what we want when we want it. However, as you grow older, your desire for intimacy overrides everything else. It is easier for you to reject sex when you are older because you do not feel an intimate connection with the partner.

Apart from intimacy, our experiences also shape our perceptions of sex. Many people have survived emotional scars from different relationships. Emotional scars do not heal so fast. They are a reminder of things that happened many years ago that you cannot let go of. For people who have emotional scars, sex might not come as easily and naturally to them as it used to. It takes a higher level of stimulation and understanding to get them to that point where they can engage in and enjoy sex once more.

The problem with having insecurities about sex is that they hold you back and prevent you from enjoying sex. You always feel awkward about yourself or the experience because of something that happened to you before, or an idea that is deeply rooted in your subconscious mind. Many people shy away from sex because of some physical flaw in their body. Each time they think about sex, they think about getting naked in front of someone, and exposing their flaws. It makes them avoid sex altogether.

There are a lot of things about our bodies that we might learn, but never control. For example, some people worry about sex because they feel they cannot control how horny they get once they are aroused. For some this might seem to be a bad thing, but for others, this is a very good thing. Having sex with a partner who readily gets aroused is something many people hope to enjoy but never really get that chance.

A culmination of personal insecurities and societal beliefs, norms and taboos results in a lot of people in relationships who are hardly getting that sexual satisfaction they crave, and instead engage in sex as a matter of obligation. This is why in many relationships we have partners who are comfortable being around one another, enjoying their company and doing all other things together apart from engaging in sex.

Because of different upbringing, some people cannot even have an open discussion about sex. To them, sex is a taboo subject and should never be talked about other than behind closed doors with their partners. For many couples, such inhibitions are the cause of the marital problems that they have. There will always be one partner who feels they are not getting as much out of the relationship as they should.

Perhaps you have a high sex drive and your partner does not, or is unaware of their level. If you cannot discuss something like this openly, the partner with a lower sex drive might feel they are being used, and probably are in a relationship with a maniac. On the other hand, the partner with a higher sex drive will feel repressed, guilty each time they initiate sex, and with time they might seek other avenues to quench their thirst.

Through this book, we try to demystify sex and the knowledge that we have gained about it over the years. Sex, especially for couples, is about two people who care for one another. What you want from your sexual encounters depends on how well you can communicate it to your partner.

We have seen many relationships that are purely functional, devoid of any element of intimacy. This is not the kind of life we are supposed to live. Sex is a special thing, shared between two individuals who value each other's opinion and attention.

When we discuss sex openly with those we love, we establish an understanding that can help us establish vibrant and healthy sexual lives.

Sex is about emotional intelligence, if you really want to enjoy it. There is so much you will learn in this book to help you overcome the possible inhibitions you have about sex. Sex is also about your willingness to explore different dimensions, explore your body, and understand yourself better so that you can teach your partner how to love you like you want them to.

Forget about all the assumptions you have known about sex for a minute. This book teaches you to approach sex from a consciously clear mind. The information in this book will help you revitalize your life. Remember that we are not getting any younger. That does not mean that we cannot enjoy the pleasures of sex and intimacy as we used to while we were younger. Right now we are older, bolder, and wiser, and we should not miss out on the cravings that we have yearned for over the years.

Chapter 1: The Birds and The Bees

Sex and sexuality are intriguing subjects that will often get different kinds of attention. Today we feel entitled, thanks to the benefits of modernization and technology. More often, we feel we are the generation that knows it all when it comes to matters sexual. Take a few friends out for pints and just as your lot is getting tipsy, introduce the subject of sex and sexuality. One thing you will realize from this discussion is just how enlightened we are.

Talk about toys and someone will mention something you probably haven't heard of or seen yet. Someone will mention a freaky style they picked up on a business trip to Thailand, another will mention something fancy their partner had them excited about the past few weeks. There is so much going on around us about sex that we might be excused to think we are the generation that knows everything about sex. Well, hold onto that thought for a minute!

The Welcome Collection features an Institute of Sexology exhibition that will challenge everything you knew about sex, especially if you believe that our generation is the *with it* generation. While we might have access to some of the most incredible and imaginative sex toys in the market, for example, exhibits in this collection are proof that we are nowhere near being the most inventive generation. There are toys in the exhibition that date back more than 28,000 years. Clearly, if we were to have a history class on the evolution of toys, your favorite vibrating rabbit might as well be the equivalent of homo sapiens in our evolutionary history.

A walk down memory lane reveals that sex toys are not a modern concept at all. They have been in existence for thousands of years. In fact, while they have served as sex aids, historically they were used as symbolic instruments used to keep evil spirits away, and to boost fertility - amazing, right? Plastic or rubber definitely were nowhere in existence back then, so as you can imagine, most of the toys were carved out of wood, stone, and in some cases, camel dung.

In fact, while the term dildo is very common today, its earliest use dates back to 1400 AD. It is coined from the Latin word *dilatare,* meaning to open wide. It is also borrowed from the Italian word for delight, *diletto.*

If we cross over to the Middle East, ancient Egyptians and the Greeks are reported to have favored unripe bananas as sexual aids. Another user favorite back in the day was camel dung coated in resin. Traders in ancient Greece sold *olisbos,* which were objects meant to help women enjoy satisfaction and achieve sexual pleasure in case their husbands were not around.

So clearly, while our generation has access to some incredible sex aids, we are not the pioneers we want to think we are. Beyond sex aids and toys, sex and eroticism have come a long way. There is a good reason why they say prostitution is one of the oldest businesses in the history of mankind. It is because for as long as we have been around, sex has been around. What might have changed over the years is our perceptions.

Perceptions around sex generally depend on your interactions, upbringing, and environment, among other things. It is more of an acquired taste. Many people hardly talk about sex, demonizing it in the process. This is not what should happen. Sex is a beautiful thing. The fact that you are sharing your intimate self with someone means a lot.

A History of Sexual Civilization

In the following section, we will discuss perceptions of sex over the years from the perspective of different civilizations. This will help us understand the history of sex better, as we build on this knowledge.

Greek Mythology

You have come across so many terms used to describe some aspects of sex and sexuality. From pederasty to eroticism, aphrodisiac and nymphomania, all these terms have their roots in ancient Greek civilization. If anything, this is proof of how much this society contributed to our knowledge of sex today.

Greek mythology is awash with tales of gods and goddesses like Aphrodite, the goddess of love. Between the 4th and 6th century, pederasty was common in Athens. Older men would have boys who had attained adolescence serve as their lovers. However, not much is known about the amount of physical sex that took place. On the other hand, women were considered more of property than willing and committal sexual partners. The younger adolescent boys would, therefore, enjoy more favor than the women in ancient Greece.

At the same time, it is worth noting that this was a society that held female prostitution in high regard. In fact, some of the high-end escorts in society were among the most powerful and wealthy individuals, in the process paying very high taxes from their profits. The flip side of a society that glorifies prostitution is that there would be a lot of unhappy wives whose needs are neglected. These wives would have to find other ways to satisfy their needs and desires. To satisfy their needs, many of the wives ended up with tribades, or lesbians.

Ancient Rome

When discussing the sexual conquests of ancient Greeks, Rome comes a close second. In ancient Rome, the man in the family owned everything. Wives and children were his belongings, just as other earthly possessions. Not only did the man own his wives and children, he also wielded complete authority and power over them. Women who were caught in the act of adultery would be punished by the husband. In some cases, the punishment was severe, and some husbands would kill their wives.

Despite these stringent measures, ancient Rome still had a thriving orgiastic culture, especially during festivals and carnivals. The Bacchanalian festivals were one such exception. During these festivals held in honor of the Greco-Roman god of wine, freedom, ecstasy and intoxication, everyone indulged in the pleasures that be, without fear of reprimand. There was no restraint during these festivals, and women would indulge themselves at will. Remember that this was also a society where a woman would risk divorce if her husband feared she drank too much wine.

There was a lot of lawlessness and hedonism associated with these festivals, with wanton sexual encounters, both of homosexual and heterosexual nature. By the time the Bacchus worship was outlawed, prostitution in Rome had spread like wildfire and it was legal. A cause for concern among the elite was when the birth rate in Rome had dropped significantly. This was widely attributed to the fact that most men engaged in pederasty. Other than pederasty, the catastrophic population decline in the Roman empire was also attributed to widespread disease and plague.

Enter the Christians

Between 400 AD and 1000 AD, Christianity was introduced to many traditional societies. With this, lessons on morality in the Christian way increased and many people abandoned their sexual conquests. Most of the laws and rules about sex in the Christian way were borrowed from the Old Testament teachings according to Hebrew law. The threat of hell and punishment from God in different forms were some of the most successful deterrents that would keep many societies in check.

Preachers reminded people that sex and lust were a result of the original sin by Adam and Eve. Those who wished to inherit the pleasures of paradise as promised by the prophets would have to embrace a celibate life, until they were married. As expected, many who wished to live a godly life embraced this lifestyle. The view of sex for ancient Christians was largely influenced by the teachings of the Old Testament. In this society, acts like anal sex, oral sex, masturbation, incest, and homosexuality were considered sinful and punishable according to the Christian doctrines. Individuals who engaged in any of these acts would be punished severely. The severity of punishment would in many cases involve both Christian and traditional laws.

The only kind of sex that was tolerated was sex within marriage. This sex was purely for reproduction. According to these traditions, sex was not meant for pleasure, but reproduction alone. In light of this, contraception was banned according to Christian law because it was seen as a means of avoiding responsibility. People who used contraception would probably be engaging in illicit sex, not for the purpose of reproduction, and more so, with other people other than their wives or husbands.

Not much is known about the influence that such rules had in the lives of ordinary people, but the risk of being ostracized from society or punished in unimaginable ways turned sex into this activity that was shrouded with danger, a lot of risk, and fear. Sex became a secret affair that would only be spoken about in private.

Even in modern society, the church is still grappling with indecision regarding sex and contraception. For the most part, the Catholic church, for example, has been against the use of contraceptives for many years. Faced with the modern world challenges of disease and the need for family planning among other issues, the church is slowly but begrudgingly embracing contraceptive use.

16th - 19th Century Europe

The church maintained a steady grip on society and many communities considered sex within the confines of the teachings of the church. However, in the 16th century, syphilis ravaged Europe. This was proof that while the church believed it was in control, the society was not as chaste as they would have made the church believe.

By this time, prostitution had become widespread all over Europe. Ancient Rome alone had more than 7,000 women who were publicly plying their trade as prostitutes, and paying taxes to the state. In London, the Southwark brothels were legendary, with their tales shared by travelers and business associates all over the continent.

However, these were interesting times and with the Italian Renaissance, naked sculptures and paintings of men and women were not seen as sinful, but as adored works of art. People worshiped and admired such art. Many of the elite in the society embraced and tolerated homosexuality.

In 1533, the Buggery Act was passed during the reign of King Henry VIII. This act defined buggery as a sinful and unnatural act of sex, which was against the will of God and man. Therefore, sodomy was punishable by death. However, this act was rarely enforced. As fate would have it, the Duke of Sutherland who was openly gay rose to power as a prime minister in the 18th Century. He, however, had to resign because of propaganda and satirical tales that were published about a gay sex club he had opened. During this time, sex had evolved from the taboo activity that was associated with guilt in the Middle Ages to a risky and intoxicating form of pleasure.

By the 19th century, ignorance and widespread gentility had turned the course of sexuality. Many people lived an ideal marriage life by the community standards. However, at the same time, they also lived a secret life of debauchery that knew no boundaries. Prostitution became widespread to a point where there were more than 78,000 prostitutes in London in 1839, in a general population of around two million residents.

This society would come face to face with the realities of careless sex. Venereal diseases were spreading at an alarming rate, especially syphilis, between prostitutes and their clients and eventually the clients' families.

Modern Sexuality

The history of sex and sexuality is full of intrigue. Today we live in a world where people are more enlightened than before. We know of the risks of unprotected sex, the benefits and joys of sex. From a young age, kids are taught about practicing safe sex, consent, and many other dynamics of this amazing act. But how did we get here? How did we get from the taboo act to this beautiful act that people talk about these days with so much admiration and anticipation?

A majority of the old ideas that society harbored about sex in the 1960s were forgotten in the face of a sexual revolution. For example, contraceptives were openly appreciated. The pill gave women more control over the repercussions of sex. This allowed them to engage in sex for pleasure, and not just for the purpose of reproduction. Many started having multiple partners in a bid to explore the pleasures that be.

Sex as we know it today has evolved so much. We openly discuss sex, especially on social media. Not much has changed about the key dynamics though. Take prostitution, for example. It has also evolved and embraced technology. Today you can easily meet someone online for casual sex, pay, and go your way. You can even leave a review.

In the household, sex is not a taboo subject anymore. With the exception of a few communities, women are no longer seen as property of the man. They have control over their bodies, and more importantly their sexual desires. Today the liberated woman is more forthcoming and opinionated about what works for her in the sack. Couples are often advised to be more open with one another and talk about what works for them regarding intimate matters. This has led to an awakening, with more people admitting their ignorance on sexual matters.

Sex education classes are a thriving business, which points to the fact that more people are interested in learning about sex and sexuality, beyond what they grew up knowing about this subject.

Changing Perceptions on Sex

As a society, there are a lot of changes that take place all the time. We embrace those that we feel are in line with our beliefs and norms, and shun those we are not comfortable with. Over the years, attitudes about sex have been changing a lot. There was a time when we had a society whose view of sex was so traditional, anything to the contrary would be considered a rebellion against the social norms.

Today things have changed. It is not just in our perception of sex, but also sexuality. A lot of people are more open to explore and discover more about their bodies and sexuality today than before. This is part of what many refer to as the sexual revolution. We enjoy more freedom over our bodies and what we want to do with them. This is particularly true for women. For years, women have been condemned to what is handed to them in as far as sex is concerned. In many societies, a woman was no more than a man's property to do with as he pleased.

Living a life of unfulfilled sexual desires meant that many women had to seek satisfaction elsewhere, either through a different sexual partner, or to find ways of pleasuring themselves personally. Even the idea of personal pleasure has been frowned upon, until now.

Today very few people get surprised when you say you pleasure yourself. In fact, a lot of people expect you to. This is quite a shift in dynamics, given that a few years ago, self-pleasure was considered more of a taboo and deviant behavior in many societies. Right now people are more enlightened to the benefits of self-pleasure, to a point where admitting that you have not done it before might even make you feel like an outcast.

There is a huge generational shift in attitudes about sex. The perceptions of young people and their parents are different. For example, in the 1970s, there was a very low acceptance rate for premarital sex. Today, people engage in sex more casually than before. Most people engage in sex to satisfy their carnal needs, and not for any attachment, emotional or otherwise. We have also seen more acceptance and support for partners of the same sex.

What we are experiencing now is a situation where people are becoming more open-minded about sex in some scenarios and a bit traditional in others. For example, today a lot of people would easily sleep with someone on the first date. The tradition of waiting a few weeks or months to go on a number of dates before you sleep with someone seems to be on its deathbed. When people go out on dates, they decide almost the moment they see each other whether they will have sex or not. Other things like the conversation, choice in restaurant, and personal grooming might only help to convince the partners, but the decision was already made when the two people met.

Sexual liberation is another issue that is worth discussing. We live in a society where people are more independent and liberated about their sexual needs. In fact, at the moment, a lot of people are growing more tolerant of promiscuity in their relationships. This, however, happens as long as the partners have a consensus on how it happens.

On the same note, more people are willing to build friendships purely on sex. Such are friendships where there is no expectation of love, long-term commitment or romance. All the participants want is sex and a good time. This might also be influenced by the *sponsor* or *blesser* culture that is currently rampant all over the world. It is a culture where older, and financially stable men and women "adopt" a younger desirable lover. The kind of relationship they have is one where they enjoy each other's company, especially for sex, while the older partner takes care of the younger partner's needs, often financially.

Let's talk about sexual exploits, for a minute. Men talk about their sexual exploits as conquests all the time. They have done this for years since civilization began. That has not changed much today. What has changed is that today, women are also openly talking about their conquests, and it is acceptable. In fact, some people even find such women more attractive and a suitable sex partner because of their adventurous nature. Women are no longer just the receivers in sexual matters, they are also givers. They take control.

Would you consider sleeping with someone before marrying them? The answer to this question some years back would be no, for a lot of people. Today, however, many people would definitely consider sleeping with their partner before marriage. One of the reasons people give for this is to make sure they know what they are getting into. No one wants to be tied down for life with a partner who cannot satisfy their sexual needs and desires. Because of this reason, sex is currently one of the things that people look for in a potential life partner.

One of the most visible changes in attitudes towards sex today is that there is an increase in explicitness when people talk about sex and sexuality. If you take a closer look at newspapers, films, magazines and novels, sex scenes sell more. They drive more conversations everywhere. When *50 Shades of Grey* came out, most conversations online were about the sex scenes.

The sex industry has also grown to accommodate these desires, such that today we can easily get erotic clothing, vibrators, lubricants and explicit videos to help people who seek satisfaction in one way or the other. With all the stimuli necessary for sexual gratification readily available, we now have a culture where sex is all around us. This also explains why it is easy to find people engaging in sex in places that would otherwise be prohibited.

What Do People Want from Sex?

We fantasize and think about sex more times than we are willing to admit. The pursuit of sex has seen many people spend countless hours chasing after someone in particular to help them achieve their goals.

Human beings are complex creatures. Just as there is no

universally accepted reason for eating French fries, there is no universally accepted reason for wanting sex. Everyone pursues sex to meet a specific reason. In some cases, we think we know why we are after sex, while we could be so far from the truth.

There are several reasons why we want to have sex. Let's look at some of them below:

Physical Satisfaction

Sex for most people is about physical satisfaction. There are quite a number of reasons behind this. More often, you want to release some tension. After a long day at work, most people get home with a lot of stress and tension in their bodies, and sex provides a good avenue to release this tension.

Another aspect of physical satisfaction is the pursuit of pleasure. That elusive orgasm almost always makes everything seem okay when you get it. Especially after an intense sexual session, achieving an orgasm together with your partner is one of the most pleasurable moments about sex that people crave.

Physically, a lot of people engage in sex because they find their partner to be attractive. An attractive partner is that person that everyone would wish to get in the sack with. If you are having sex with an attractive person, chances are high that you feel very good and confident about yourself.

There are also some people who engage in sex to improve their skills. Of course, they have many other physical reasons for having sex, but one of their goals is to learn how to become better and refine their love making skills. In this category, we have those who seek sex from escorts and prostitutes hoping to learn new tricks they can use to impress their loved ones. This particularly applies when they feel their partner is more experienced or adventurous, and they would wish to match that energy.

Personal Achievements

A lot of people pursue sex as a means of achieving some personal goals. More often, such people use sex as a weapon, even though some are oblivious to this. You only realize later when you have achieved so much that you can use sex to get you anything you want. We have come across many people who achieved their social status and wealth through sex. It brings them closer to authority and power, and it becomes so addictive, they cannot stop.

As social beings, we are constantly worried about what people think about us. Social status means a lot to us, even when we cannot admit it openly. Mind-blowing sexual encounters with persons in authority usually elevate partners to a higher social standing, which gives them confidence about their lives.

One of the darkest personal achievements that people seek in sex is revenge. This is more common and happens especially in committed relationships. Perhaps one partner happens to cheat and the other finds out. There is a lot of turmoil after such findings, and once the aggrieved partner finds peace, is calm and collected, they make a conscious decision to seek revenge sex so their philandering partner can also feel the same pain they felt.

Emotional Satisfaction

Beyond the physicality of sex, it also has a strong emotional appeal that a lot of people seek. Many people have sex for love and commitment. By giving themselves to someone, they hope to get the same feeling reciprocated. In some cases it doesn't work, and this can cause a lot of pain and despair. Without reciprocation, you are left wondering whether you are okay, or if your partner even finds you attractive in the first place.

Sex is also a means of expressing oneself to their partner. In as far as communicating between romantic partners is concerned, those who have perfected this level of communication often find it easy to understand one another.

Insecurities

Personal insecurities have led many people to have sex, in many cases with the wrong person. Your personal insecurities are an individual problem. Seeking redress through sex from the wrong people will hardly ever give you the satisfaction you need. A lot of people who struggle with esteem issues will try to boost their esteem by having sex with someone. They hope to feel better afterwards, but the gains are short-term. Instead, you should address the deep-rooted reasons for your esteem issues and insecurities.

Another form of insecurity that people try to overcome through sex is to comply and do whatever their partner wants. In many cases, you engage in sex either under pressure or because you feel it is your duty to satisfy your partner's needs. At this point, you engage in sex not because you need to, but because you are afraid of the repercussions of not pleasing your partner. This level of control is common in unhealthy relationships.

Many people engage in sex to prevent other people from pursuing their partner. This is a form of mate guarding that is common especially in colleges among young people. Once you are intimate with someone, you can make a point of letting other people know so that as word goes round, people who were interested in your partner will avoid them. It works in some cases, but not all the time. This is because most of the time you assume that other people are interested in your partner, ignoring the possibility that your partner might be interested in pursuing someone else to satisfy a curiosity.

What Do People Really Want From Sex?

What we have discussed above are classifications of some of the simple assertions we can make about our pursuit of sex. When we compare sex between men and women and their desires, there are significant differences in the behaviors and motives behind sex. The most important thing is that you first perform a needs assessment on yourself. A self-exploratory approach will help you understand the reasons why you seek sex when you do.

In human psychology, sex is one of the most underrated facets of human well-being. There are many assumptions we make about sex that result in skewed perceptions of why we are having sex or not. For men, the biggest assumption is that sex is a need, irrespective of where, who or what they get it from. For women, most of the time sex is about love and intimacy.

Fundamentally, all humans are wired to seek comfort by meeting their psychological needs. In the same way we strive to

24

meet our basic needs of food, shelter, and clothing, we also pursue psychological needs in that manner, even without knowing it. We need to satisfy these needs to live healthy and stable lives.

Over the years, psychologists through different studies have categorized four fundamental needs that we pursue in life:

- Self-esteem

- Security

- Connection

- Autonomy

To live a happy life, we must meet each of these needs regularly. Without them, our minds are programmed to find ways of meeting them, in many cases, at the expense of anything and anyone that stands in our way.

To meet these needs, we come up with social and psychological strategies. Some of these strategies might be devious but as long as they help us achieve our goals, we are happy. Many experts believe that sex is not a need, but a means to achieve our psychological needs. The reason for this is because to date, there is no tangible proof that asexuality or celibacy are unhealthy psychologically or physically. What this means is that no one has ever died because they did not have enough sex. If we look at the possible risk exposures to having sex, you might even argue that there are a lot of health benefits of abstaining.

However, we are not saying you should not be having sex. Sex is amazing. It makes you happy and healthy and is one of the most affordable stress and pain relievers you will come across. The truth is that over time, humans have evolved to learn how to use sex as a means of meeting psychological needs instead of physical needs.

Much of the misunderstanding about sex comes from the fact that men and women pursue different things in sex. The needs they seek to satisfy are different. Many years ago, the easiest way for a woman to secure a solid future and get healthy babies along the way was to marry someone who was by society's standards, a successful man. Therefore, sex was more of a means to security. While a lot has changed today, the appeal of a secure, successful man makes him a suitable partner for many women. They seek stability.

For women, it has not been an easy ride through history. Their sexual needs and desires have often been suppressed and shot down. As a result, many women grow up to have a confusing relationship between their need for self-esteem and desire for sex. For this reason, it is easier for women to go for sex to satisfy the desire for belonging or to find a connection with someone because for the longest time, they have been trained and conditioned to feel awful if they seek sex for any other reason, especially for personal gratification.

The case for men is different. A lot of men use sex as a status symbol, especially amongst themselves. If you manage to have sex with a lot of women, especially those women who many men feel are unattainable or out of their league, you are seen as a conqueror. Tales of your exploits are almost legendary. Because of this reason, a lot of men are conditioned to pursue sex to satisfy this desire to boost their ego among their peers.

Since we are all traditionally conditioned to pursue sex for different psychological needs, it is usually difficult to understand one another. A lot of partners struggle with this because each one feels their needs are not being met the way they should. This also explains why some women feel men are desperate and insecure about sex, while men on the other hand, feel women are manipulative emotionally and clingy.

Men and women both need to find avenues for personal, independent development away from sex. This way, they can both free up sex and use it for intimacy. When you develop independent of each other, you recognize your strengths and weaknesses in the right places, instead of using sex to fill the empty slots in your self-esteem. As you establish healthy connections with people and institutions around you, you will barely feel the need to compensate through sex because you feel unattractive in some way.

If you can take care of your psychological needs through different approaches like a healthy social life, successful professional career, or a healthy and loving family, then you will be in a good position to approach sex from an attractive place, not as a needy person who is compensating for their shortcomings.

When we lose ourselves in our pursuit of our needs, we often project our frustrations on the people around us. Sexual intelligence is not just about sex, it is about what we feel about ourselves on the inside. It is about those conversations we never have with ourselves or our partners. It is just nature!

Chapter 2: What Are We After Here?

Every society has social norms that define interactions, and sexual norms are high up on that list. This is because sex has a special place in society. Have you ever wondered for a minute whether your sexual activities are normal? Granted, you get pleasure all the time, but do you ever wonder how people would react or respond if they found out what you do, and that it makes you happy?

When discussing sexual norms, some of the common topics that people discuss is how often a normal person should have sex, what kind of sex you are having, or your fetishes. None of this is something to be embarrassed about. Questioning your sexual behavior is also a normal thing. Many people do that. The most important thing is for you to understand that this is what you love, and it works for you.

We live in a world where many people are sexually depressed, so the fact that you are liberated and understand what works for you is a good thing. This allows you to communicate your needs to your partner. Once you understand one another, it is easy to satisfy each other, and live a happy and fulfilling sexual life.

At each stage in life we have unique preferences about sex and sexuality. Some of the things you enjoyed five years ago might not really impress you today. Our needs and attitudes change with time, so you should not feel bad about something you used to like but don't get excited about anymore. Besides, we live in a society where people are more open to talking about sexual activities and behavior today than ever before, even though for most people, these are still viewed as private affairs.

The Concept of Normal Sex

Something interesting about sex though, is that while you might be excited about the prospect of normal sexual behavior, experts advise that from time to time, deviating from the norm might actually work well for you. It might lead you to a path of sexual discovery where you will unravel interesting things you never knew about your body and your sexuality. Let's discuss some of the things society considers normal about sex today.

How Often Are You Having Sex?

The question of how often you are having sex is everywhere. People frown upon those who supposedly have very little sex just as much as they do those who they feel are having too much sex. This begs the question, therefore, how much is too much?

To answer this question, we must first understand what your perception of sex is. In your opinion, what do you consider as a sexual encounter? In this case, we might consider oral sex, vaginal intercourse, and mutual masturbation. Whichever one of these that you consider as a sexual encounter works for you. Generally, many people consider penetrative sex as the epitome of an encounter. Therefore, this is what they consider when discussing how frequently they have sex.

It is safe to say most people who live a more reserved sexual life will only consider vaginal sex. However, if you are an experimental person, what works for you is anything that stimulates you and makes you feel good. In this case, masturbation and oral sex count just as much as vaginal sex.

There are other dynamics that come into play too when discussing the frequency of sex. For example, marital status. There is a common myth that married folks have more sex, probably out of obligation or because they have each other. However, many married couples will admit that this is not always the case. There are a lot of issues people deal with in marriage that make it difficult for them to keep the fire burning as much as they would love to. Sex is one of the reasons why some couples end up in marriage counseling. It gets to a point where one partner feels the other does not reciprocate their sexual attention as much as they would wish for.

Single people or individuals who are in non-committed relationships seem to have more sex than everyone else. After all, they don't have to worry about the obligations that come with sex. It is as simple as feeling the urge and finding someone who can satisfy the urge. Other factors that determine how much sex you have include health and age. Very few people manage to stay as energetic about sex as they were in their younger years.

So what really is the benchmark for how much sex you should have? To be honest, there is none. Sex is not about widely accepted norms. It is about you and your partner. For the most part, it is about you. Your partner cannot satisfy you if you do not understand what you want. Having an open discussion with your partner about what turns you on and how many times you need their attention will help you get closer to appreciating your needs better. When you are with someone who understands you and knows what you want, it is not the frequency of sex, but the quality that matters.

What Kind of Sex Are You Having?

Sex is not just about that single act of penetration, or that style you fancy. In a survey conducted by the National Survey of Sexual Health and Behavior, respondents suggested more than 40 sex acts. Of course vaginal penetration is the most popular, followed closely by oral sex and partnered masturbation. From this combination alone, you can tell that everyone has a different view of sex, depending on what works for them. While partnered masturbation, for example, can be openly discussed, many people cannot discuss individual masturbation openly. They get pleasure from it, but it is one of those things that people are very shy about.

Other than the type of sex you are having, the other issue is whether you prefer intercourse with a condom or not. When it comes to condom use, other than preventing unplanned pregnancies and the risk of infection, many people who use condoms have just as pleasurable an experience as those who do not.

In some communities, using protection with your loved one is frowned upon, because others might suggest lack of trust in the relationship. However, condom use is normal and acceptable even with your loved ones, if you talk about your reasons for using condoms. Most of the misconceptions and misunderstandings about condom use arise in the absence of honest conversations about it.

Orgasms

An orgasm is one of the most elusive conquests in sexuality, especially for women. It is unfortunate that many women get through life without ever experiencing an orgasm, or knowing what it is about. The orgasm in most cases is an assumption. For the men, they assume they deliver the best sex their partner will ever receive. Therefore, they assume that their partners have orgasms each time they have sex. On the contrary, many women admit to faking orgasms when having sex with their partners.

Vaginal sex will in most cases result in an orgasm for men. Others get orgasms from oral sex and other forms of stimulation. For the ladies, however, things are different. Experts believe that women get more orgasms when other forms of stimulation apart from penile penetration are involved.

One thing that remains a fact is that every woman has a different trigger that arouses them to orgasm. There is no one-size-fit in female orgasms. In this case, therefore, the concept of normal doesn't apply.

Too Old for Sex

There is a misconception that sex is a preserve for the younger generation. This is not the case. In fact, sex is just as important for people older than 40 as it is for people in their twenties. Quality sex actually has a positive impact on life after 40.

There are different sexual activities that people engage in as they grow older, which deliver the same level of satisfaction as intercourse. Hugging, caressing, touching, and anything intimate helps them feel important and loved. Sex is one of the last things anyone would willingly give up just because they are growing old.

The four categories discussed above are issues that you will come across often when talking about sex. You will realize that what society considers as normal might not always work for you. The most important thing about sex is to understand your personal desires and those of your partner. That level of understanding strengthens your intimate bond, and helps you appreciate one another.

The Concept of Sexual Taboos

The moment we talk about what society considers normal in sexuality, it follows that we have to talk about the things that society frowns upon. Sexual taboos manifest in different ways. In many cases, there is a fine line between normal and taboo, given that over time, we are learning to embrace different sexual acts.

Oral Sex

We are supposed to enjoy sex, but unfortunately, not everyone does. People have different reasons for holding back. Perhaps you are not with the best or right person, or maybe you are afraid you might embarrass yourself in the process. Oral sex is one of the subjects that attracts a lot of controversy. Some people treat it with contempt, but others embrace it fully.

Oral sex is one of the ways you can achieve an orgasm. It is pleasant, especially if and when done in the right way. You have to set aside your fears, relax, and allow yourself to enjoy it. Of course there is the benefit that both partners might achieve an orgasm, without the risk of getting pregnant, for ladies.

The concept of a taboo behind oral sex for many people comes from previous bad experiences. It is difficult to enjoy something when each time you attempt, you recall memories of the last time things didn't go according to plan. To be fair, oral sex is not necessarily a taboo because it should not be done, but because of lack of communication.

It is more of a personal taboo than a societal taboo. It is one of those choices that people make as a personal choice because perhaps they don't feel happy about the way their partners respond, or how they perform it to them. The secret to overcoming this is to explain to your partner what you feel they are doing wrong. Teach them how you want to be loved, how you want them to pleasure you orally. It is in this way that we turn things around and start enjoying oral sex as we should.

It is also important to remember that when having sex with your partner, it is not all about you. It is about both of you. Everyone tries to figure out what the other person likes best. It is about the gestures they make, their body movements and so many other things. You need to feel good and satisfied. If you understand what your partner enjoys, you too can feel satisfied and enjoy the moment.

The beauty of oral sex, especially for ladies who do not get excited very easily, is that it can serve as foreplay. Take note that this is not to substitute penetration, but it helps you get your mind prepared. For a lot of ladies, stimulation takes place in the mind. Oral sex helps you get that awareness that you are about to do something awesome. It helps you enjoy the experience.

In case you are about to have oral sex with your partner for the first time, try and relax. You might both be under a lot of pressure to get it right. This will get on your nerves and you will struggle to get it right. There is nothing wrong with experimenting. Forget about everything you have heard or read about oral sex before, and focus on this one moment. No one is perfect, and there is no perfect way of getting oral sex right. You try, and listen to your partner, and together, you will realize what works for both of you.

One thing you will realize about oral sex is that it gets you out of a comfort zone, and opens up your sexual world to new realities. It is actually one of the most sensual things you can do to one another. Oral sex is one of the sexual acts that has enjoyed quite the revolution over the years, so that very few people consider it a taboo anymore. In fact, you will be surprised to learn that more people are getting satisfied by oral sex alone, even without penetration. It strengthens your confidence, relationship, and more importantly, makes you and your partner more intimate.

Period Sex

Believe it or not, period sex divides opinions everywhere. Some people appreciate it, others loathe it. For the most part, opponents of period sex argue about discomfort especially because of the mess. The decision to engage in period sex depends on what both partners are comfortable with.

Interestingly enough, there are a lot of women who enjoy having sex while on their period. It heightens their sexual excitement, and makes them feel desirable and loved. If someone finds them attractive enough to want to have sex with them during their period, then they clearly are quite the catch.

After all, who else would tell you had period sex, other than your partner and yourself? For guys, if you don't have reservations about entertaining a woman regardless of the blood, you might actually enjoy this. The taboo-ism around period sex is more about personal choices. As long as you are both comfortable with it, go ahead.

Masturbation

When was the last time you talked about masturbation with people around you? It is a subject that is spoken about in hushed tones. It is an act that many people feel embarrassed to discuss openly, yet they perform it in the privacy of their homes or anywhere else they feel they need to get off.

Masturbation has for a long time suffered because of religious condemnation. Many religious teachings against masturbation argue that it encourages people to engage in pervasive sexual acts, promiscuity, and hinders self-control. After all, all you need is to think about it and go on. Some of the traditional religious groups actually consider masturbation as a moral disorder.

Another reason that contributes to the stigma around masturbation is the kind of upbringing that people have. When you are brought up to see masturbation as a sin, you cannot see it any other way. It might take a while for you to even consider it, and when you do, the guilt often makes you feel worse after. Everyone has sexual thoughts and feelings from time to time. Without a way to express these feelings, you can become frustrated with life.

Masturbation is not just something you do or enjoy on your

own, you can also enjoy it with your partner. Self-stimulation can help you learn more about your body and the things you like. It makes it easier for you to communicate with your partner and let them know what you prefer, and how.

The interesting thing about masturbation is that while society outwardly considers it a taboo, many people still perform it anyway. There are lots of health benefits from masturbation, which explains why more people engage in it today than before. Here are some of them:

- **Pain relief**

Orgasms and sexual arousal induce the body to produce oxytocin, a chemical that acts as a pain reliever. This act will, therefore, help you reduce muscle pain, headaches, and might even help insomniacs get some sleep.

- **Stress relief**

If you have had a difficult day at work, school, or in whichever engagement you are committed to, masturbating at the end of the day could help you relax and sleep peacefully. Besides, the body produces endorphins during masturbation. These endorphins help to improve your mood, and might even help you fight depression.

- **Sexual satisfaction**

You do not necessarily need to be in a relationship to enjoy the pleasures of sexual satisfaction. All that sexual tension piling up in your body is not good for you. According to experts, men who masturbate frequently have a lower risk of getting prostate cancer.

- **Improve your health**

Masturbation can help you improve your health in different ways. It improves your immune system, which will generally help you have a healthier life. Besides, you can also learn how to prevent premature ejaculation. Masturbation is more of an exercise. If you can learn to last longer when on your own, you will probably also last longer when you are with your partner.

- **Body exploration**

Women have always had the wrong end of the deal when it comes to sexual matters. In many societies, exploring your body is seen as a taboo. This is why a lot of ladies go through life without being able to enjoy the pleasures that lie within.

Masturbation helps ladies explore their bodies, in the process understanding themselves even better. Since you know what works for you, it is easier to advise your partner on how to make love to you, which will benefit everyone involved.

Looking at all these benefits that you stand to gain from masturbation, perhaps it is time to reconsider the whole taboo agenda. However, we must also take note of the fact that masturbation is only helpful up to a certain point. You must have your limits, or it could become an addiction that threatens to derail your life.

Body Exploration

How many times do women refer to their private parts as *down there*? Many women who do this are shy and cannot be specific about what they refer to. They cannot say vagina or any of the other terms that define their sexuality without feeling uneasy. The shyness does not just end with their inability to refer to their privates using the right terms, it also extends to the fact that a lot of women don't know how they function or even what the parts are named.

Most of these challenges come from personal upbringing. It depends on the lessons parents, guardians, or teaches gave the girls while growing up. The lessons you learn about sexuality as you grow up stay with you for a long time. It is not easy to change some of these perceptions.

As you grow older, you get through life assuming a lot of things about your sexuality. You find yourself in a position where you can hardly speak about your sexual fears, needs, or desires with your partner. In the long run, the assumptions also affect your ability to enjoy the intimacy of sex with your partner because you believe you should never ask for something. This explains why many women are condemned to sexual frustration, unhappiness, and many marriages suffer.

Is this problem permanent? No, it is not. The solution for you lies in rethinking your beliefs and everything you have learned about sex and sexuality since you were a child. More importantly, you need to make a bold choice and learn more about your body and how it works. In as far as personal beliefs are concerned, you might need to consult an expert to walk you through it. However, what you can do on your own is body exploration.

Body exploration is not really a preserve for women. There are a lot of men out there whose knowledge of sex and sexuality is wanting. It is, however, easier for them to explore their bodies

39

because all their important organs are external. For ladies, there is a lot more exploration involved.

The simplest way to start this is to stand in front of a mirror and admire your body. As you do this, focus on your fingers gliding all over your body. Do this slowly and let yourself appreciate what the touch feels like. Start with the vulva, then if you have pubic hair, the soft mound of hair that is exposed, and finally, your vaginal lips. There is so much you can learn about your body through this exploration that will help you understand where your pleasure zones are, the perfect rhythm for you and so on.

Why is body exploration important? Many people assume that everyone orgasms through penetration during intercourse. This is not true. In fact, a lot of women achieve orgasm through stimulation. It is also worth mentioning that while it might take a man roughly three minutes to achieve an orgasm, it takes women on average 15-20 minutes just to prepare for penetration alone. Interestingly though, women's orgasms can last longer and they can enjoy an orgasm even three times longer than most men enjoy theirs.

While you can approach body exploration on your own, it is also something you can try with your partner. Someone who cares about you wants to know how you like to be touched. They want to know how you love to be kissed and stroked, because these things are important to achieving your ultimate satisfaction. Where possible, guide your partner on the best way to pleasure you. Fix your gaze on their eyes, but take their hands on a guided tour of your body.

Sharing intimate information helps you clear any

misunderstandings that might prevent you from enjoying one another's company. It will also help you clear the air about what your expectations are. In as much as exploration is important, remember that open and genuine communication with your partner will make this more intimate and pleasurable for both of you.

Sexual Position

We all have one or a few sexual positions that we love. However, not everyone enjoys them as much as we do. Men can experiment with a lot of positions and still have fun while at it. For women, things are a bit different. There are some positions that everyone seemingly enjoys, but are not as comfortable for the ladies.

Believe it or not, not every woman likes to go on top. This is one of those discussions that people barely have. What do you do once you get on top? Do you move up and down, from one side to the other, do you jump or squat like you are at the gym? Many ladies who are not comfortable about their bodies in particular, find this position awkward.

Let's talk about the other one, reverse cowgirl. So you turn around and all you have to look at is your partner's feet, *yikes!* You are having an intimate moment with your partner and while they have their full gaze on your body, all you have to look at is their feet? What kind of atrocious wizardry is that? Other than the awkward moment where you have to stare at your partner's feet, a lot of women worry about breaking the penis if they make an abrupt turn.

Forget about everything you have seen in the movies, shower

41

sex is not as easy as they make it out to be. It is, in fact, one of the most difficult positions to hack. Why do the movies have to lie so much? You have a lot of concerns while attempting this. Thinking about your posture, stability, what if you slip and break a hip, or worse, what if you slip and smash your head on the floor, ending up in the emergency room or the morgue? These are some concerns that make a lot of people coy about some sexual positions that would otherwise be considered the in-thing by many people.

Anal Sex

For the most part, discussions about anal sex have often been initiated by men in the relationship. This is one of the taboo topics in sex that a lot of people are uncomfortable with, and for a good reason. When you mention anal sex, one of the first things that comes to many people's minds is that you watch too much porn. After all, that is the one place where people seem to engage in anal sex without questions asked. Many people see the anal area as a part of the body whose specific role is to expel body waste. Therefore, this is an exit. For entry, go round the other way.

As would be expected, many homophobes will widely reject the idea of anal sex. The reason for this is because they feel when you accept anal, you are slowly graduating from a heterosexual to a homosexual. It doesn't matter whether you try it with your heterosexual partner, to them it means there is nothing stopping you from pursuing anal sex with a member of the same sex. Therefore, anal sex for them is not a heterosexual act. As you would imagine, most of these sentiments are from men.

Interestingly enough, women who agree to or even love anal sex share different views on this. One of the most important things according to the women is that the decision to receive or give anal is a personal choice. There should be no coercion involved.

In a world where people are sexually liberated, independent and willing to try new things, there is a growing number of partners who are open to trying anal sex. Many who have tried it do believe it delivers a unique sense of pleasure on its own. There are different dimensions of anal sex that must be considered.

First, when giving anal sex to a man, you have direct access to their G-spot. You can stimulate them in the same way that men stimulate women. There is also the element of power. In a normal heterosexual encounter, the man is in a position of power over the woman by virtue of the fact that they are penetrating the woman. When they engage in anal sex, the woman gets to experience what it feels like to dominate their partner the same way they get dominated.

Besides, the fact that anal sex has always been considered a taboo makes it one of the things that our generation is overly interested in trying out. To be honest, beyond the conversations that people have online and in public, a lot more people are trying out and enjoying anal sex than they are willing to admit, perhaps for fear that they might be seen as sexual deviants.

The thing about sexual taboos is that with time, they are becoming more relative. To be fair, no one has the moral authority to tell you that what you are doing in bed is wrong. As long as you are not doing anything that would be considered illegal according to the law, go ahead and have some fun.

Conversations around sex used to be taboos, but today we openly talk about sex without flinching. It is like the conversations that people have about cannabis today. More and more people are opening up to different possibilities and you cannot help but share your experience with others.

If you are an adventurous spirit, many of the things that would be considered taboos will probably be on your bucket list, crossing them out one by one. Besides, most of the practices considered as taboos are either prohibited as a result of societal or religious pressure. None of that has anything to do with your intimate needs. Our world has changed and more people are opening up to new experiences about sex. You might just find the best thing in your sex life when you explore. Remember that as long as you are consenting adults, what you do together in the name of sex is between the two of you. Religion or society has nothing on you.

Exploring Intimacy With Your Partner

A lot of people cannot tell the difference between sex and intimacy. In fact, we often confuse the two. It is possible to have and enjoy sex with someone or your partner without being intimate with them. Common examples where this is possible include a one night stand, sex with an escort, or friends with benefits. These are examples of sexual acts where there is no intimacy or feelings involved. Fair warning though, most people assume that friends with benefits is purely about sex, but after a while, feelings get in between and the sex becomes intimate, at least for one partner. The thing about such sexual encounters is that there is nothing about them that breeds trust, comfort, or warmth. They are purely about taking care of your sexual urges.

Intimacy is different from any of these encounters because when you are intimate with someone, you need to know them deeper and allow them to know you deeper as well. It is like taking a guided tour through their soul. You cannot get intimate with someone you just met at the bar, or when you are having a quick romp in the back seat.

Intimacy is an interesting aspect of a relationship because it takes a very long time to nurture. The duration before you can claim to be intimate with your partner is also not universal. Some people get intimate within the first few weeks, others take longer. What happens is that there must be a sense of trust to enable you open up your world to someone.

However long it takes for you to be intimate with your partner, you must be gentle and patient. You should not come in with expectations. There are a lot of mistakes that might happen along the way, but it is important to learn how to forgive those mistakes. You are learning to love your partner the way they want to be loved, and this might not be the easiest thing to do.

A lot of people long for and seek intimacy but they never get it. The reason for this is because many of us are in a hurry. We approach such situations with a checklist and if we do not find what we want, we move on to something else. To be honest, getting close to another human is not one of the easiest things to do. You open up your life to them, your insecurities. You show them your vulnerabilities, hoping they can return the favor and show you theirs too.

45

You have a lot of fears that you should work together to overcome. As you discover the important things in each other's lives, your intimacy matures to a point where it becomes a love language. The fear you once felt when opening up about the things you worry about turns into trust and adoration. You look forward to the loving gaze in your partner's eyes when they hold you close.

So what really is involved in intimacy?

- **Knowledge**

When you are intimate with your partner, you know them beyond the basics. You know what matters to them deep down in their hearts. They don't have to spell it out for you all the time. You can tell from their body cues that something is not right.

The level of understanding you share with an intimate partner is that which cannot be taught anywhere. In their hearts you found treasure that you would not wish to find anywhere else. Because of this, you can put up with the few differences between you guys, and learn to embrace your diversity.

- **Appreciation**

Embrace one another and accept your differences. These are the things that make you who you are. You don't always have to share the same passion with your partner. You can, however, respect the things that they love, and their reasons, just as you would expect them to do for you. One of the most beautiful things about relationships is that as you discover your differences, you learn how each of you is unique. This also gives you a good chance to explore a new world that is important to your partner.

• Acceptance

One of the biggest mistakes that people make in relationships today is to try and change their partners to suit their preferences. When you get intimate with someone, you accept them as they are. You love them for who they are. Of course, there are a few changes that people can make in their lives, but not the fundamental ones. When you pressure someone into making such changes, you simply push them away because you are trying to turn them into someone that they are not.

• Compassion

Problems arise all the time in relationships. How you work through the problems is what makes the difference between an intimate relationship and any other. When problems arise, you should address them in a compassionate manner. Do not blame your partner or shift goal posts. You are part of a team, so work together towards realizing your team goals together. More importantly, remember that you are working towards the same goal, not competing against one another.

• Security

Do you feel comfortable enough to be vulnerable with your partner? This is the real definition of intimacy. When you open up and let your partner see your weaknesses. You pull down your defenses because with this person, you feel safe and protected from the rest of the world. Intimate partners celebrate each other's strengths and encourage them to be better where they fall short. You feel comfortable that your partner respects the decisions you made together, and none of you will violate the mutual understanding.

- **Emotional security**

Intimacy between partners grows stronger when you share an emotional connection. There will be times when you have a lot of problems that need to be addressed. To do this, none of you should feel like you are walking on eggshells around your partner. You should not have to choose your words carefully, or hold back from saying what you really wanted to talk about.

How to Build Intimacy

Now that we know what it takes to be intimate with your partner, how do you nurture intimacy? Where do you begin?

The first step is to choose the right partner. This is someone you will give yourself to fully, without holding back. Many times we choose the wrong person to commit to and struggle to understand why they never reciprocate our love, affection, and attempts at intimacy. If you realize that to be with your partner, you have to give up everything that you enjoy, everything that defines you, then this is not the right person for you.

If you are with someone who makes you feel awkward about sex and your sexuality, who blames you when they are not satisfied, or always says you are not doing enough to pleasure them, perhaps it is time for you to walk away. You should only make yourself available for someone who appreciates you the way you are.

If you are getting into a new relationship, remember that it needs room for growth. As the relationship grows, you will learn a lot about one another. You will figure out some of the things that you find attractive about your partner, and the same applies to them too. You should allow yourself room to express yourself in terms of your beliefs about sex and your sexuality. Talk about things with your partner, things that are important to you. When discussing these opinions, remember that each of you probably believes in something different. This should not be a problem for you. To nurture intimacy, allow yourself enough room to learn more about your partner's desires, just as much as they will learn about yours.

You are in different relationships with different people. The relationships you have with your friends, family members, colleagues, your kids and so on, should be different from the intimate relationship you have with your partner. There are different ways you can choose to define what works for your sexuality with your partner. This is important, so that you know where to draw the boundaries. This will also help you determine what makes your relationship different, special from every other interaction you have with people.

You should learn to be mindful about your partner's emotions as they too should be about yours. The thing about sex with someone you are intimate with is that every session means something. Therefore, even if you only get in the sack with your partner for a few minutes, it is enough time for them to realize when something is not right. They will notice when you withdraw, when you are not yourself, and more importantly when something is bothering you.

You might feel angry about different things from time to time, disappointed, or hurt. These are the things you should talk about. Sex is not supposed to be a weapon you use to control your partner. It is something you share passionately with the one you love. If you realize that you are withdrawing from your partner, work with them to overcome those fears. Perhaps one of you is having a difficult time at work, and the pressure is spilling over into the bedroom.

Conflict is a part of relationships. There will be conflicts all the time. You should never ignore conflict, especially when it concerns your sexual relations. Without addressing conflict, you are creating a platform where each of you will build up your anger over certain issues and explode when you cannot hold it any longer. When you are intimate with someone, you must find a way to address your issues together courageously. You should have faith in your ability to work through it, and support the relationship irrespective of the kind of crisis you are dealing with.

More importantly, for any healthy relationship, you have to learn to be the kind of partner you expect your partner to be for you. There are two of you in this, so no one should feel like they are putting in most of the work. Sex is often the breaking point in many relationships. When one partner feels they are not getting enough, it gets to a point where they cannot keep suffering any longer and seek pleasures elsewhere. It gets worse when they step outside and meet someone who makes them feel better than you ever did. At such a point, resentment creeps into the relationship, and you will hardly ever be the same again.

If you need your partner to be a compassionate, generous lover, you should also make an effort to return the favor. It might not be easy, but together you can learn each other's love language. When you are intimate with someone, you must go out of your way to make sure you are worth their intimacy. They give themselves to you fully, so it is only fair that you do the same. If you or your partner fails, give them feedback in a loving way so they can learn and do better next time.

Chapter 3: Great In The Sack!

What makes you crave sex? What is it about you that makes you desirable to your partner? There is a lot that we think we know about sex, but that does not really matter. We know many people who claim they are sexually satisfied and living very happy lives. At the same time we also know those whose sexual lives are filled with frustration. So what is the difference between these two groups?

Many who are living happy and fulfilling lives sexually are at a level of sexual intelligence that most people don't identify with. The first thing you learn about sexual intelligence is that it has nothing to do with your predatory seduction skills, or your physical appearance. Sexual intelligence and satisfaction are about some important skills that you might learn or improve on over time.

Whether we believe it or not, sex plays an important part in our lives. You need to be emotionally stable about sex, or it can override and ruin your life. Sex is a very powerful thing and most people just aren't aware of how powerful it is. Dissatisfaction and frustration are common when your needs are not being met. But how do you get to that point? What do you do to get out of it and overcome the frustrations?

Most of the challenges we experience about sex are in the absence of sexual intelligence. This happens because of prejudice and ignorance. There are many things about sex that we assume we know and others that we take as the gospel truth because that is how they were handed down to us. The majority of these concerns arise in the form of religious beliefs and widespread myths concerning sex. To help you overcome these challenges, you must first be open to learning. Armed with the necessary knowledge, you can refute claims and myths around sex for the hoaxes that they are, and instead embrace a happy life based on factual information.

Let's use a simple example to explain this - the orgasm. Men and women have different perspectives of an orgasm. For most men, an orgasm culminates in ejaculation. This might not always be the case for women. For the ladies, an orgasm might proceed beyond ejaculation into caressing at the end of intercourse, or eroticism. As we mentioned earlier, orgasms are different for each woman. The definition and how different women arrive at an orgasm are not the same.

The biggest issue we have with sex is that a lot of people have no idea what their bodies are about, or how to respond to different stimuli in their immediate environment. It is because of this reason that they often feel ashamed or embarrassed when encouraged to explore their bodies and learn more about themselves. Therefore, when we talk about sexual intelligence, we need to think critically about ourselves. Ask yourself what is it about your sexual relationships that you are not happy about? What do you need to feel fulfilled and satisfied? When we ask and answer such questions honestly, we become open to experimentation and exploring the erotic possibilities that lie ahead of us.

While learning about ourselves, we must also work towards enhancing our communication skills so that we can tell our partners what we need, what they are not doing right, and how to improve. Two of the most important things concerning sexual intelligence are proper communication with your partner and trust. Trust allows you to release control of your body to your partner, so they can take care of you and pleasure you. Trust builds intimacy between partners and strengthens the bonds of your relationship. This is how you can find common ground with your partner and enjoy your sexual experiences better.

Intelligent sexuality involves establishing a connection with someone. You must make an effort to interact with someone. This level of interaction goes hand in hand with trust, because you open up about your sexual life with your partner. By doing that, you welcome them into your life and share in your experiences. It is about being honest not just with your partner, but also with yourself. You present yourself as you are, so they accept you in similar fashion.

Many times we look at sexuality in terms of our sexual organs and forget about the most important organ, the brain. You have to learn to be creative, to move away from all the traditional ideas you know about your body. For mutual appreciation, you must love your body as it is before someone else can love you as you are. When you do, you are comfortable in your body as it is, and see yourself as a complete sexual being that is lovable and adorable.

One mistake many couples make with sexual relations is to introduce power struggles. Sex is a powerful thing that a couple can share. However, when you turn sex into a power struggle, the intimacy behind it fizzles away. It becomes about who is better than the other. This kind of competition is not good for the relationship. Granted, we have made many mistakes in the past when it comes to sex. This does not mean we cannot undo the mistakes.

You can make changes, improve your sex life, and enhance your sexual intelligence. The good thing about mistakes is that if you are willing to learn from them, you can change a lot of things in life. Talk about your fantasies and desires. Discuss the things you crave so you can release yourself from inhibitions that prevent you from enjoying an amazing sexual life, like guilt and mistrust.

If you want to enjoy your sex life, you must come up with a mutual manual that works just for the two of you. This is a process that involves both your participation. The first thing you must get rid of is the concept of anything goes. Don't just give in to something because your partner wants it. If it makes you uncomfortable, let them know. Try and understand why they want it so badly, and together, you can arrive at a worthy compromise.

The other thing you need to let go of is the notion of perfect sex. We cannot all give great porn-star sex. It is almost impossible. Even porn-stars do not get it right all the time. It takes a lot of cuts that never make it to the final scene for them to achieve their goals. If you have been reading or watching a lot of Kamasutra, you need to take a break because no human is perfect. Some of the positions described in such literature require a specific level of fitness and physique to accomplish. Without that, you might always feel you fall short when in a real sense, you are attempting the impossible.

Emotional balance in sexual intelligence is an aspect that we can culture slowly through responsibility, respect and sensitivity. You should not look down on your partner just because you have had more or better sexual encounters than they have. Do not frown upon their mistakes. You might have had some negative experiences with sex in the past, but this is not something you should dwell upon.

More importantly, where there exists love, admiration, and appreciation of one another, sex is more enjoyable, happier, and healthier.

Importance of Knowledge in Sexual Intelligence

There is a lot we assume we know about sex but in reality, we don't. Most of the information we know about sex comes from what we learned in school, while growing up or through our peers. How much of this information is true is a matter of perspective. However, we use it to define our sexual relationships, and the impact they have on our lives and whether we will enjoy sexual satisfaction is incredible.

When we get information about sex from the wrong sources, it affects our ability to have a stable and normal sexual relationship, especially with someone who has the right information. More often, you will feel as though your partner is imposing on you but in the real sense, they are trying to enlighten you.

As we grow up, we should be able to make important and healthy choices about sex with a clear mind. There are so many things that you should learn about sex. This should help you explore different beliefs and values that you have known about sex, and other important subjects that you might come across in the near future. Through this, you learn how to get through social relationships and manage your personal sexual health appropriately.

Parents, for example, play an important role in the knowledge that their kids learn about sex. It is important for any parent to make sure that they teach their kids the right way. Some parents shy away from important subjects and their kids eventually learn from the wrong places. By this point, their view of sex and the parents' view of sex are not the same.

Some of the things you need to learn about sex include the following:

- **The human anatomy**

You might be surprised, but there are many people who do not know how the sexual system works. Everything from sexual orientation, reproduction to their gender identity is a challenge. Learning about this helps you to relate with people comfortably, because you understand them and respect them for who they are.

- **Building healthy relationships**

The kind of relationships we have with people around us will have a significant impact on our sexual lifestyle as we grow up. You should try and foster healthy relationships with your family members, your friends, and romantic partners. You might not have met your soulmate yet, but each relationship you find yourself in should teach you one or two things about having a healthy sexual relationship.

- **Communication skills**

How well you communicate with your partner will also determine the nature of your relationship. Many people are in relationships where they hardly ever get things done for them the way they want to. This is because in their relationships, they never learned how to communicate what they want.

Sex is an interesting faculty. Many people work with what they get. If you do not communicate effectively, your partner might end up ignoring your needs innocently because they are not aware. Before you learn how to communicate your needs to your partner, why don't you take a step back and learn how to communicate with yourself? This is where many people go wrong.

You have to know what you want. You must know what works for you and what turns you off. These are some of the important things that will help you stay enlightened, and discuss your needs with your partner.

An important aspect of communication is negotiation. There are times when you will need to learn how to negotiate for better or more in the relationship. If you feel your partner is going overboard and you are not ready for that, instead of shutting down or lying down quietly in compliance, you should voice your concern in a good way. Let them know they are moving too fast, and you cannot keep up.

Besides, you will not always be ready for sex all the time. When this happens, your partner who feels they are ready might be left heartbroken when you turn them down abruptly. Learn how to read the mood, so that even if you are not ready, you can turn them down politely or postpone the moment for later. The older we get, the more our responsibilities demand of our time. It will, therefore, be difficult for you to keep up all the time. However, if you can communicate this effectively, you should not have a problem.

• Sexuality and sexual behavior

When it comes to sexuality and sexual behavior, you should know what it means to abstain and why it is important. You should also learn about how your choices affect your partner. This is a level of sexual intelligence where you step out of your cocoon and look at things from the perspective of your partner. Some of the decisions you make in life regarding your sexuality will go a long way and might affect your relationship if you are not very keen.

This is also the point where you open up about infections, the use of contraceptives, and pregnancy. For the most part, many guys leave these discussions to the ladies. A lot of men barely know what contraceptives their partners are using and why. What other options do they have? Why do they choose what they choose and not the others? Have you ever visited the fertility clinic with your partner? Do you see the doctor with them or you just wait for feedback when they come back?

• Cultural affiliations

Your community will always have an impact on what your views on sex are. This is because it is how you were brought up. There are different roles expected of everyone in the relationship, especially when it comes to sex. There are some things you expect a man to do, and others you expect of a woman in the relationship. All this, however, is a matter of perspective, and in some cases principle depending on how you were brought up.

Remember that you will come across a lot of information in the media about sex. Some of this information might influence your thoughts about sex and sexuality, but you have the power to choose what persuades your ideas.

The Value of Emotional Health

One of the most difficult conversations you can ever have with yourself is about your sexual relations. Everything gets blurry when you take a critical view of your sexuality. You might even feel uncomfortable thinking about your sex life. Because of such inhibitions, a lot of people are unable to enjoy a happy life because they cannot move forward when it comes to sex. You find yourself stuck in a place where you can neither define what makes you happy nor what doesn't. As a result, you willingly receive whatever is given to you.

You need a high level of emotional astuteness to help you understand what your sex life is about. You might even be afraid, thinking of what the dreary journey into your sex life will be. Most of these inhibitions can be traced back to family settings, cultural, and religious teachings about sex. The kind of judgement and persecution that you learned when you were young about being honest and direct about sex might be stuck in your mind, keeping you from pushing through the barriers.

Another challenge many people have is that when we start talking about our sex lives, we have to open up and expose ourselves to things that we are unsure about. You are not just worried about feeling ashamed about the sexual acts you think of, or what people might think of you, but deep down, something you learned when you were younger makes you feel guilty and it prevents you from exploring your sexuality. Because of this reason, a lot of people are often reluctant to talk about or even think about their sex life, especially when it involves looking back to some of the things they did back in the day. However, remember that your sexual experiences define you and make you the person you are today. Whether they were good or bad, there were important lessons you learned from them, and these lessons should be a stepping stone for you to build a happy and fulfilling sexual life.

So, what should you do to exercise emotional maturity and be an adult about your sex life?

A lot of people are in a position in life where they might as well be unconscious about their sex lives. The reason behind this is often assumed under adult responsibilities, but this is not always the case. The fact remains that responsibilities will always be there. However, you should also learn to find a way to open up and allow yourself to enjoy sex more. The problem here is that we assume that sex is a routine. Like any other routine, it should flow naturally even without you putting in some effort. This is where we go wrong. Speaking honestly about your sex life will help you overcome the aspersions you have about it.

If your desire is to have a life filled with sexual energy, and a happy, fulfilling life, you need to learn how to talk openly and think about your sexual life. This is what will make your relationships better and more fulfilling. Think about sex as you would any other aspect of your personal development, from spirituality, your career to emotional well-being. You have to put in the work. Sex deserves just as much attention as every other aspect of your life. If you do this, you will realize that over time, your sexual life improves and you feel satisfaction from every encounter, however brief it might be. Many people spend countless hours having sex but never feel satisfied. They are left empty because in the first place, they do not know what they are looking for. You have to make a conscious decision to step out of your sexual coma and pursue a new sexual life.

The cost of social consciousness might be too high for many people to pay. You have to be honest about your fears, fantasies, thoughts, and feelings. This will also help you overcome previous nasty experiences. You need to regain your sexual freedom and learn to be more aware about what your body needs. If you continually use sex as a means of escaping some of the things you should be dealing with, you might struggle to reconcile some of the important issues in life.

Awareness of your emotional health gives you more control over your life. You get control and freedom over psychological trends and patterns that influence your decisions. You are able to avoid sexual experiences that might not be suitable for your lifestyle. You learn how to respect yourself and your desires. If you have had terrible sexual experiences in the past, emotional maturity helps you learn how to avoid getting into the same predicament. You make conscious decisions about your sex life and who you want to enjoy it with.

It does not matter whether you are in your 20's or 50's, whether you are married or single, what is more important for you is to ensure you are on the right path to sexual growth. With the necessary support, you can explore what sex means to you in an objective way. You can think about sex independent of the influence of other things like drugs and alcohol. This is because you can have an honest conversation about sex and your relationship with yourself.

In case you are in a relationship, you should think about the kind of conversations you have with your partner about sex.

You should also think about what you communicate without having sex. Discuss how these issues affect your self-esteem and confidence around one another. You will learn so much, especially about how your fears about being inadequate affect your life.

Be gentle in this approach, and ask your partner what they feel about sex, your sexual ability, and what you can do together to improve and have a good and satisfying experience. Most of the difficult conversations that involve sexual awakening are not easy to start, but once you can have them with yourself, you can open up and do the same with your partner. The effect is amazing, and will help you set yourself free from the old patterns that threaten to derail your happiness.

Understanding Your Body

There is so much that we assume about sex, especially when it comes to the female anatomy. The female body, for a lot of people, is full of mystery. The female body does not just baffle men, even a lot of women are often left surprised by how much they have yet to learn about their bodies. The fact that most of the female genitalia are hidden away from sight, unlike men's, adds to the puzzle of female pleasure mechanisms. Therefore, every woman has a different approach to pleasure.

There are many guys out there who cannot correctly identify female sexual parts, as there are women. One of the reasons for this is because the female anatomy has not been studied as much as the male anatomy. One of the challenges with this predicament is that we do not even have sufficient scientific information about the female anatomy.

It is much easier to find information about male genitalia everywhere, even in the media. Male genitalia is widely used, especially in the media, references in pop culture, or even in slang jokes. This persistent use makes a lot of people familiar with the male genitalia. Perhaps one of the other reasons why the female genitalia doesn't get much attention is because of the culture of inhibition and tabooism that has often been associated with female anatomy. People can openly talk about male anatomy, but when it comes to female anatomy, many people shy away.

The challenge for women is that it becomes difficult to understand what their bodies are about, unless they go the extra mile. Many women also end up conforming to societal norms, and find it uncomfortable and a taboo to talk about or even ask questions about their anatomy.

One report suggested that more than 70% of women can correctly identify male genitalia. However, barely a third of the same population can correctly identify at least six parts of their sexual anatomy. It gets worse, as a lot of single women surveyed in Taiwan in 2014 did not understand what it meant to have sexual desires. Perhaps this can be attributed to their inability to understand their anatomy.

One of the most important things you need to do is to understand your body in order to fully experience your sexuality. The fact that many women do not know what their sexual anatomy is about, or the functions of their genitalia, means that it is difficult for them to achieve an orgasm. This is because the location and function of the clitoris and vagina are related, and determine how often they can get an orgasm. If you cannot identify them, it is difficult to tell whether you know what your sexual desires are, and how to achieve them. It also becomes difficult to discuss sexual desires with your partner because you have never known what it is about.

By taking the extra step to understand your body better, you will find it easier to enjoy sexual satisfaction on your own. Other than that, it is also easier to do the same with your partner because you can guide them and help them learn your body and what works for you. Unfortunately, a lot of women never get this chance.

We cannot peg our hopes on sexual education to help us understand our bodies. This is because there is a lot of misleading information out there. There are many women who have over the years received inaccurate information about their sexuality, which they assume is the correct information about their sexuality. Many societies, especially those that are traditional and believe promoting knowledge on female genitalia might result in promiscuous behavior, tend to conceal a lot of information from girls when they are growing up. In some cases, all the information the girl child gets comes from her aunties and grandparents, most of whose idea of sex education is largely flawed.

Other parents and caregivers do not believe they need to teach their daughters about sex. One of the reasons for this is because as they grew up, their experiences with sex were different, and the topic was largely a taboo. Therefore, they do not see the need to impart useful knowledge to their daughters or sons for that matter. They hope that the learning institutions will take care of that for them. This is the same kind of upbringing that makes it difficult for many parents to have an honest and candid discussion about sex with their children.

For this reason, a lot of people advance into adulthood unaware of what their sexual anatomy is about. They don't know how to take care of their sexual desires and any other important information regarding their sexuality becomes a myth. Most of the sexual education that children get comes from their learning institutions. If the teachers are anything like their parents, they are either poorly trained, or embarrassed to even discuss sex and sexual organs with the students. Besides, many teachers lack the necessary tools to teach young boys and girls about their sexual anatomy, so we end up with a lot of children who mature into adulthood with misinformation or no information at all about their sexuality.

Enter the Internet, and this is where most young adults go to find information about sex and their sexuality. While the Internet has been a great source of help for many people, it is also one place where information is not controlled. Therefore, it is not easy to tell what you can learn online. Besides, the fact that information about sexual anatomy is available online does not mean that it is also readily available for everyone. There are many parts of the world where access to the Internet is still a myth, let alone access to electricity.

A big reason why it is not easy for women to discuss their bodies is because society has for a long time emphasized innocence in a way that makes many people lead inexperienced sexual lives by not knowing anything about their bodies. How do you achieve an orgasm? If you ask many people this question, you will be puzzled by the responses you get. Many people do not even know what an orgasm is. For men, a lot of them are wired to believe that sex ends when they reach their orgasm. This can also be attributed to porn culture. Most of the films young people watch end when the man achieves his orgasm, completely ignoring the needs of the woman.

The good thing about our modern society is that we are more receptive to new information and challenging the conventional myths. Today more people are willing to talk about their sexuality than before. People are getting more comfortable with discussing female anatomy, its functions, structure, and orgasms in public than ever before. These are the conversations that are helping what we have largely referred to in this book as the sexual revolution. We are not there yet, but the progress we have made is commendable.

For example, many people will fondly talk about the sex toys they have at home, and how much pleasure they get from these toys. Such discussions were never easy to come by a few years ago. This points to a dynamic shift, where people are open to exploring their bodies and sexuality on their own. Many others admit to using toys with their partners, without the act of sexual penetration. This has helped them realize there is so much more to their sexual anatomy than they have known, and there are limitless boundaries to which they can push their sexual desires.

Why Should You Explore Your Body?

There are many benefits of exploring your body, either on your own or with your partner. Many women who set aside time to explore their sexuality have healthier, better sexual lives and marriages. They are also more confident than their peers who are relatively coy about exploring their bodies. We can attribute this to the fact that these women have the best understanding of their bodies and their sexuality. With this knowledge, they are able to improve their sex life with their partners, too.

The benefits of the ability to express yourself sexually don't end there either. You will also see the following changes in your life:

- You enjoy quality sleep
- You feel younger and more vibrant
- You have a high chance of living longer
- You have a low risk of depression or cancer
- You have a better chance of improved fertility

The beauty of understanding your body is that the benefits are about more than just improving your sex life. One of the key reasons for learning and understanding your body is to help you know how to take care of yourself. Simple things like hygiene can be elusive when you do not know what you are working with. A lot of people who never learned about their sexual anatomy struggle to take care of their bodies. This can be quite a frustrating experience when they meet sexual partners who are very particular about genital hygiene.

From such experiences, many people feel embarrassed about their sexuality and even think of themselves as too dirty to warrant any sexual attention. Such thoughts linger on for a long time, and make it difficult for them to live a happy, normal sexual life. Therefore, learning about your sexuality and understanding your body is more than just getting knowledge, it is about empowering yourself, building your self-esteem around your body, and making you confident. With society loosening its grip on the stigma around the female body, we can look forward to a world where people are sexually empowered and understand their needs better.

Chapter 4: Becoming A Better Lover

What makes you a good lover, or better than the last person? Everyone believes they are the best there is at sex. After all, you try your best to impress. Unfortunately, many people are nowhere close to being the lover they believe they are. The good news is that all is not lost just yet. Even when you are not at your best, or if you are out of touch with what has worked for you for a long time, you can still find your way back and manifest your ultimate sexual power.

The first step is to completely become one with your body, and be in the moment. The interesting thing about sex is that it is very easy to tell when someone is withdrawn. You can feel they are far away, their minds preoccupied by other things apart from the act of intimacy. This becomes a problem because your partner feels they are not special anymore. They feel you are with them out of obligation or you are probably thinking of someone or something else. It can be so demeaning, especially when someone gives themselves to you fully.

There are things we do, at times unconsciously, that prevent us from enjoying the best of sex with our partners. One of these is fixation on things that do not matter, like performance. You are having a good time with your partner, then all of a sudden your mind wanders off, thinking about your performance. Are you good enough? Is your partner enjoying the moment? Are they faking? Such thoughts prevent you from focusing on the most important thing that matters at that moment: your partner.

You might be having one of the best sexual sessions you have had in a long time, but the moment your mind drifts away, the passion dies. It gets even worse when your partner realizes you are not with them in the moment. It is important that you learn how to exclude such thoughts and focus on the beautiful moment you share together.

Staying in Control

To enjoy the best of sex and become a good lover, you must realize how to control yourself and control the moment. This kind of control is not just about you, it is about your partner too. More importantly, it is about that intimate moment you share. To enjoy sex, you must embrace the power within it. You must embrace the sexual energy and share it with one another. Many times one partner might feel they are doing too much while the other is just fine.

Staying in control is about more than just controlling the sexual encounter, it is about realizing where your true power lies, and how to share it with your partner. Remember that sexual power is not supposed to be used as a weapon to conquer, hurt, or manipulate your partner. It is something sensual that should be shared. When you share your passion and power with your partner, they open up, relax, and give themselves to you willingly.

Think about it for a moment: how would you feel if someone intentionally made you feel less of a partner when having sex with them? The power you wield when having sex transcends what you do in bed. It is about how comfortable you make your partner feel. Do they feel safe with you, loved and appreciated? It is a special connection that transcends the physical aspect of sex. This level of control helps your intimacy.

70

If there is one thing about sex that works for a lot of people, it is when you figure out a way to connect your spirituality and sexual power. It makes intercourse more amazing, sensual, and satisfying. The only challenge is that many people struggle to achieve this. We are shrouded by a lot of problems all over, caught up in a world that is too busy that we forget about the need to live the full experience of our lives. We just keep getting by, surviving instead of living a normal, happy life.

When you connect with someone on a higher level, the kind of satisfaction you get is unique. It is the kind of satisfaction you enjoy from an intellectual perspective. You open not just your body to sex, but your spirit, too. It does not matter whether you are enjoying this kind of sex with your partner or on your own, you unlock dimensions of sex that many people can only dream about. This is the kind of sex you enjoy without inhibitions.

One of the key tenets of becoming a better lover is emotional intimacy. Emotional intimacy is one of the most beautiful things you can share with your partner. It is a bond that binds you to your partner in a way that you feel comfortable, loved, and special whenever you are together. This is what makes the difference between normal physical sex and making love. You might be surprised how many people out here who cannot tell the difference between making love and having sex.

We derive emotional intimacy from shared feelings, affection, and being comfortable enough around someone to allow them to experience our vulnerability. It helps you empower and reinforce one another's attractiveness in a way that makes you feel special whenever you are together. Whether you are together as friends or lovers, you share a special bond of trust that helps you see one another in a different light. You do not just see your idea of the person you are with, but you get to experience them in their full sexuality. You embrace them and become one with them. Because of this, in the face of anger, conflict, or any feelings and sentiments of hurt, you commit to working with them through it.

So what really makes you a better lover? Couples that are in tune with each other's needs usually have something unique about them that they keep going back to all the time. There are things about your partner that remind you of how much they mean to you. This includes things like the way they kiss you, the way they touch you, their voice or their scent. Below are some qualities that you might possess which increase the likelihood you are an amazing lover:

- Your willingness to learn more about your partner and the things that they love.

- You are passionate and playful when you are alone with your partner.

- Each time you are around your partner, you make them feel comfortable, secure, and sexy.

- You open your world to your partner so they can experience your vulnerability, but at the same time show them that regardless, you are confident as you are.

- You are an adventurous spirit and always willing to try something new or experiment.

- You are a good listener, and go out of your way to communicate your needs to your partner.

- You never rush when enjoying pleasurable moments with your partner. You take your time. Sex to you is not a destination, it is a journey, and you come prepared for a long journey.

- While you enjoy receiving pleasure from your partner, you also enjoy giving it back in kind.

- You do not judge your partner. You listen and support them.

- When you are together, you blend in and become one in your intimate moments. You make and sustain good eye contact and do not want to let go.

These are some of the things that make you a better lover. Most of these are universal. There could be others that are not on this list, but are unique to you and your partner. It is important to find those things that you both enjoy, that bring you closer together, and build on them. Those are the things that make your bond stronger, and your sexual life better.

What Makes Us Poor Lovers?

While we know what we can do to become better lovers, it is also important to discuss a few things that we are not doing right in the relationship, which are pulling us away from our partners. At times, the answers we seek are not in the things we are not doing, but those that we are doing wrong.

- **Personal Inhibitions**

Many people struggle with personal inhibitions about sex and other things especially regarding their partners and their bodies. We discuss inhibitions at length in this book, and hopefully, you realize that most of them are just imaginative concepts. Some inhibitions have nothing to do with us, but the kind of upbringing we received while growing up. You can overcome them and turn your sex life around.

- **Lack of Time**

Time is another constraint that prevents many people from enjoying their sexuality with their partners. We can dedicate a lot of our time to improve our lives, careers, and so many other things, but when it comes to our sex life, we become lazy. Many times people claim they are too tired, do not have time, or many other reasons to avoid spending time with their loved ones.

It hurts so much, especially for women, when they take their time and prepare everything, set aside a special time to enjoy with you, but when you get home, you cannot spare time to be with them. Such behavior makes someone feel inadequate, or doubt whether you find them attractive anymore. When doubts start creeping into your sex life, you either find a way to solve them immediately, or they persist and kill the fire in your sex life.

- **Self-centeredness**

Sex is not just about you, it is about you and your partner. Many people are selfish and only care about their needs. The biggest culprits in this are men. Most of the time men barely put in the work to please their partners. You come in, romance for a few seconds, have sex and crash on the bed and fall

74

asleep. This usually leaves your partner wondering what just happened? That was it? When you are done before your partner even gets ready, it leaves so many questions lingering in their minds. It feels like they are being used as tools to satisfy your desires, but theirs are ignored completely.

Sex and intimacy are about understanding. You should not just jump in, pull a few strokes in and call it a day. The romance and pleasure before penetration are important to your partner because it prepares them psychologically for what is to come. Remember that many women take much longer to be ready for sex, some even close to 20 minutes or more. If you are done in 5 minutes, you hardly care about their needs. It might even get to a point where your partner comes up with reasons not to have sex with you, because they don't feel their affection and sexual desires are reciprocated.

- **Technique**

Indeed, missionary is one of the easiest positions out there, but it is not the end all in terms of techniques to use. There are many other positions you can try. The conversation about positions is one that you should have with an open mind with your partner. You can learn a lot together, so try and find out what works for you.

More often, we limit ourselves to the few things we can easily do when sharing intimate moments with our partners. The problem with this is that it soon becomes boring, and you might even believe you cannot try something new. Other than sex positions, your technique when making love to your partner should not be limited. Try a different tempo, rhythm, and new ideas in the bedroom. Try sex in different places in the house. Send the kids away to their grandparents for a weekend and just get crazy all over the house. It might come as a surprise to you, but you might just realize how freaky you guys can be.

- **Turn Off Your Mind**

Mental distractions are quite a turn off. Your partner, who has been with you for years, pretty much knows when you are in the mood or not. When your mind strays, they feel it and wonder what or who you are thinking about. When this happens, even your performance is affected. You seem distant, unbothered, and it feels like you are just having sex as an obligation. You want to get it done and move on to other things. This can be quite disturbing for many people.

A lot of us are guilty of this problem. You come home to your partner but carry the baggage of the day with you. Your partner does everything possible to make sure you enjoy the moment, but you just cannot turn off your mind. Things that happened during the day have no place in your bedroom. If anything, if you feel bothered by something, talk to your partner about it. Tell them what is on your mind that is keeping you from focusing on them. Subtle conversations can help you ease out of your pressures and get your mind back in the game. The problem is that many people just can't bring themselves to talk about the issues they are worrying about, and it affects their intimacy.

- **Am I Sexy Enough?**

A lot of people struggle to let go and see themselves as sexy and lovable. One of the reasons behind this is because the media gives us a specific idea of sexiness. For ladies, you are conditioned to believe that a certain type of skinny is the ultimate sexy. For guys, you feel that if you do not have the Cristiano Ronaldo body, you just don't cut it.

The person you are with is with you because of who you are, not who you think you should be. If we all could be with the people we think we are or those we think we should be, we would all be Brad and Angelina. Obviously, that's not real life.

You have to first appreciate yourself the way you are, because your partner does the same too. If your partner has the wrong ideals about your body, then that is a different conversation you should have altogether. The problem with such imaginary ideals of the perfect body is that they make us view sex as a performance instead of an intimate exchange between lovers.

What really is the ideal definition of sexiness? Is there anything like a universal benchmark for sexiness? Since many people were not taught to accept themselves as they are, it becomes difficult for them to appreciate their sexiness. They feel they fall short, and will always feel insecure about their bodies. Besides, we get embarrassed to utter words like penis and vagina. This is what society has conditioned us to. Since we embrace shame all the time, we keep worrying about things we should not, while in the real sense, we are perfect just the way we are.

Emotional Intelligence Is The New Sexy!

Nothing turns people off more than someone who is oblivious of their effect on others, someone who is not sure of themselves, especially when it comes to sexual relations. We live in an age where many people have experimented and tried so many things and relationships, that when you are with your partner, you need an assured lover.

High emotional intelligence works for a lot of people, especially women. A man who is assured and aware of his sexual environment is quite the catch! This carries on into our relationships, too. You need to learn how to relate with your partner with the right amount of self-regulation and self-awareness. This will help you establish a steady connection with them, which will help you foster a lasting relationship. Even if you are just going for a fling, you will have the time of your life.

Emotional intelligence involves identifying and managing your emotions and those of other people around you. You become aware and attune yourself to what they feel. People who lack these skills will often end up in situations that they never should have been in, but somehow find themselves in and cannot get out. This is how you end up dating a certain caliber of partners, and wonder why you keep struggling to find different people out there. The challenge here is that instead of using your heart and head to make decisions, you let your emotions cloud your judgement.

People with healthy emotional intelligence can relate to others better and create good and strong connections. Most of their conversations center around finding a common or shared understanding, with constructive criticism and very few arguments. The good thing about emotional intelligence is that you become a self-motivated person. You do not need someone around to help you determine what you want. You know what you need, where it is, and how to get it. Your ambitions and goals in life are about you and they are separate from your ambitions and goals in life as a couple. You grow together independently and as a couple.

If you do not develop this skill, you will hardly be as motivated as you should without your partner around. More often, you flake on doing things you should because you need your partner's assurance before you can proceed. You end up living a passive life and things will hardly ever fall in place for you.

When you have high emotional intelligence, you are more likely to be an attractive partner because you know what you want in life, and you do not shy away from going after it. You are also an empathetic person, such that you try to connect with people whenever you can, and enjoy their company. Your interest in people around you is genuine.

Building Your Emotional Intelligence

The good thing about emotional intelligence is that it is something you can learn. Today, many of the top CEOs in the world and entrepreneurs visit coaches to help them learn how to connect with people around them. This means that you too can learn self-awareness, empathy, motivation, self-regulation, and other important people skills that make you more attractive to your partner.

There are three simple ways you can build your emotional intelligence and have a chance of living a happy and sexy life:

- **Become Self-aware**

You can learn self-awareness either through a life coach or by reflecting on your life. The secret here is to learn the things that motivate you to do the things you do, or say what you say. You can start by making peace with yourself and enjoying the quiet moments you can spend on your own. Use them to meditate and reflect on your life. If you can, write down what you feel on a daily basis and the actions that you take on those feelings. With time you will see a pattern in your thoughts and actions, upon which you can review and learn how to become a better and more lovable person.

- **Motivation**

What do you want from life? What do you want from your sex life? You need to have a clear picture of where your relationship is going, and make subtle changes regularly that will help you improve your life. Consider some of the discussions you have had with your partner before, especially about the things that you should change to improve your life. Instead of waiting for wholesome changes, take action right away and get back control over your sex life.

- **Learn to Empathize**

People skills are important if you are to rebuild your sex life. Things do not always go according to plan, and for this reason, you need to find a way to balance your needs and desires with your partner's. Learning to empathize means that you will listen to and pay attention to your partner's needs so that you understand what they need from you.

You have to be compassionate about the conversations you have together, especially about your shortcomings or their insecurities. It might be a slow process compared to the other two above, but it brings you closer and strengthens your bond and intimacy.

Chapter 5: Lose Your Inhibitions

Sexual inhibitions are more common than we can admit. Even individuals who are sexually enlightened will from time to time feel inadequate for different reasons. The problem with inhibition is that it hurts your ability to engage in a healthy relationship with anyone. More often you question yourself about whether your desires are warranted or not. Instead of opening up and talking about what you want, you withdraw, comply, and take whatever is handed to you.

There are many people who are in sexual relations where they know what they want and how they would like it done to them, but they cannot ask for what they want. Many people have this negative or frightening idea of sex that was passed down to them either by their parents, guardians, or the community they were brought up in, especially the church. The situation is so bad that in some cases, something as normal as asking their partner to touch them sexually or hold them a little longer seems like an unapproachable subject. Because of these inhibitions, you might even struggle to pleasure yourself because you are afraid of everything that you have been told about sex over the years.

To develop sexually and rediscover yourself, you must first learn to set your sexuality free. If your inhibitions are as a result of things you were taught, you need to unlearn them. Confront the ideas in your head with real, tangible facts and you will realize that none of that was true in the first place. There are a lot of things that parents teach us about sex and sexuality so that we can avoid engaging in sex earlier than they expect. It is common for many parents to use the element of fear on their kids, oblivious of the damage that this does to them as they grow up.

If you can free yourself from the sexual inhibitions, you can transform your sexual life and live a happy and content life. How do you tell you have some inhibitions about sex? Take a simple experiment when watching a movie or show on TV. How do you react when they show a sex scene? If you find yourself turning away, or shying away from the scene, this might be a sign you are not comfortable with certain activities.

Some of the sentiments that you might experience if you have inhibitions include the following:

- Feeling that scene is disgusting, wondering why anyone would be comfortable doing that in the first place.

- Doubting whether anyone would be willing to try what you see in that scene on you.

- Worrying about your religious beliefs and what people would think about you if they learned you entertained some of those desires and thoughts.

- Feeling uncomfortable and unpleasant when you watch the scene.

These are some of the things that you experience that might have you thinking about your inhibitions. If you take stock of everything you feel uncomfortable about, you might just realize how much you have been taught to ignore or reject explicitly or otherwise. These are the messages that have been wired in your brain over the years, making you think about sex as a dirty act.

82

Learning about these inhibitions is one thing, acting on them is a different story altogether. The fact that you know what you are concerned about gives you a good starting point. Beyond your experiment with the TV scenes, let's try another one, at work. Say you open your email and you receive this book attached. What do you think your colleagues would think of you if they came across you reading this book from your email? What would they think about you if they noticed you liked a social media page about sex? Better yet, how would you feel if your partner found out you were reading this book? Would you hide the fact that you are reading it or would you encourage them to read along?

Sexual inhibitions manifest in different ways. Most of the time, you worry about what people will think about you when they learn about the things you enjoy. As a result of such fears, you end up afraid to explore your body and find out more about your sexuality. This way, you end up limiting yourself.

Sex and intimacy are not things you should be afraid of. These topics are not taboo subjects. Gone are the days when people were ashamed to discuss sex and intimacy. Today you are encouraged to discuss them openly especially with your partners so that you have a better chance of enjoying one another's company. Talking about the things people are afraid to talk about helps you see things from a different perspective.

The first step towards overcoming your sexual inhibitions is to allow yourself to think about them and talk about them. You must make peace with yourself, your interests, passions, desires, and fetishes. Once you accept them, it is easier for you to talk about them openly.

We are sexual beings, so it is a pity that people do not wish to talk about sexuality openly. These are personal battles that people have on a daily basis. You feel shortchanged in a sexual encounter but cannot talk about it for fear of reprimand. You are afraid that your partner might see you as a slutty partner for asking them to pleasure you in the right way. There is a lot of sexuality bombarding us everywhere we go, from the media to our phone screens. We consume a lot of sexual content on a daily basis. Therefore, we should learn to open up and talk about things we are passionate about.

You have to allow yourself to acknowledge what you feel, the things you know, and what you want. The unspoken rule that sex is a taboo subject is not valid anymore, not in this century. You deserve to be happy, and your partner deserves to experience the best of you as you share passionate intimate moments together. Once you are comfortable in your sexuality and your body, you will find it easier to open up and be comfortable with your partner appreciating your body.

Forget about that routine, uninspiring, boring, and lazy sex life. Forget about coexisting. It is possible for you to rekindle the fire in your life that made you enjoy a happy sexual life before. You can get your spark back if you want it. In the section below, we will discuss some of the common inhibitions that prevent a lot of couples from approaching and enjoying sex.

Effect of Emotional Scars

We struggle through a lot of emotional scars in life, and many of them influence how our lives turn out. Performance anxiety, normal stress in life, physical pain, sexual dysfunction, childhood trauma—all these are some of the things we go through in life that might leave us nursing emotional scars for a long time. There are many traumatic experiences we go through in life that affect our sexuality and our ability to enjoy sex altogether.

Experts believe that people who have been subjected to some form of trauma in their life usually have a difficult time having a satisfying sex life as they grow up. This can be attributed to two things, mindfulness and psychological distress. If you have emotional scars, you might experience psychological distress more frequently than someone who doesn't, in the form of anxiety, worry, fear, or any other negative emotion through the day.

As these emotions manifest, your mindfulness diminishes to a point where you are hardly aware of the things that are happening in your life at the moment. You get so lost in your pain that your life just passes you by. This is one of the reasons why you struggle to enjoy sex.

To deal with the psychological trauma, many people come up with avoidance mechanisms to avoid confronting the unpleasant experiences. As a result, their attentiveness diminishes as their awareness of their environment does. When your mindfulness numbs down, you hardly become receptive to sexual stimuli, and it is for this reason why you end up living a life where you don't find joy in sex. In fact, most people who nurse emotional scars find sex to be unsatisfying, empty, worthless and unpleasant. They usually participate because they feel it is an obligation, not that they have something to enjoy in it.

So how do we overcome this?

It is possible that your ability to be fully present in your senses is affected by the trauma you experienced earlier. If you are struggling to enjoy sex because of such experiences, it is important that you see an expert and talk about mindfulness and your emotions. Instead of avoiding the emotions and the negative feelings they evoke, you should learn to embrace them and deal with them.

When you do this, it is easier for you to detach yourself from the pain and enjoy your life without inhibitions. This will also help you overcome many of the terrible experiences that you have had around sex.

By improving your level of mindfulness, it is easier to redirect your focus from the negativity that you are afraid of, towards your partner and the sentiments that you experience during intercourse or when you are having amazing intimate moments together. You can then look forward to having quality and satisfying sexual encounters with your partner. You will soon learn how to tune your mind to sexual cues like seeing your partner naked.

Body Consciousness

The image you have in your head about yourself can really mess with your sex life. This image gives you an idea of someone that you think you should be, but you are not. As a result, you end up feeling insecure about your body, and this will in effect prevent you from getting aroused. We usually assume that only women go through this, but body consciousness affects men just as much as it affects women. However, the effect on sexual performance or the ability to enjoy sex is not as significant in men as it is for women.

86

One of the biggest challenges that keeps many women from enjoying sex and being responsive while at it, is the perception of a negative body image. There are two ways that body consciousness affects people.

- **What you think of your body**

If you feel unattractive, you will never see yourself differently even if someone tells you otherwise. This also affects your confidence and self-esteem, and will certainly erode sexual pleasure for you. The moment you are unable to enjoy a single element of sexual satisfaction, everything about sex becomes unenjoyable to you.

Since you don't feel comfortable in your skin, you will hardly enjoy orgasms, arousal, or feel your body is desirable. As you criticize your body, your anxiety grows and you feel uncomfortable when someone touches you. Over time, your body learns to ignore sensual and sexual touch altogether.

- **What you feel others think of your body**

If you feel that your partner thinks you are attractive, your sexual performance is higher because you are confident they love your body just the way it is. On the other hand, if you feel otherwise, even when the proof points to the contrary, this will affect your desire, and capacity to enjoy sex. You might even struggle to be aroused.

Take the case of menopause, for example. While the reducing libido can be attributed to hormonal changes, many women lose interest in sex because they feel they are no longer desirable. Therefore, other than the hormones, what turns them on is the thought of being desired.

There are a few things you can do to remedy this situation. First, listen to your partner and believe them when they tell you they love your body, and you are attractive. Try and avoid negative conversations in your head especially before, during, and after sex. Calm your inner voice and remind yourself that you are beautiful and perfect. This makes it easier for you to bond with your partner since you both enjoy the moment.

Clear your thoughts. Mindfulness is a good way to do this. Clear the negative thoughts from your mind and embrace positive thoughts. Do not judge yourself in the process. One other thing that will help you overcome these challenges is to focus on your partner. Focus on their body rhythm and motion, their facial expressions, and lose yourself in the pleasure such that your bodies move together in rhythmic fashion.

Discomfort Around Other People

There are many people who struggle with the fear of being touched or touching other people. This fear is known as Haphephobia. It is not quite common, but when it comes to sexual relations, it can destroy your lives. Haphephobia is a specific phobia whereby you are afraid of being touched by anyone. However, there are people who only fear being touched by members of the opposite sex.

The challenge with Haphephobia is that people around you or strangers you interact with on a daily basis might struggle to understand what you are going through. When someone offers or attempts to touch you and you reject them, they might feel shy or unwanted, unaware that you are suffering from a condition that you might not know how to handle either.

There are different reasons why you might be suffering from Haphephobia. One of these is trauma as a result of sexual assault in the past, or some other form of trauma. We also have cases of Haphephobia where individuals just develop the phobia without any familiar cause. If your case of Haphephobia developed as a result of a specific cause, exposure to the trigger might send you into relapse at any point in life.

Fortunately, with or without a known cause, it is possible to treat Haphephobia successfully so you can have a normal, happy sexual life. Many people who struggle with Haphephobia can still foster warm relations with people around them. You can love and be loved. However, the problem is that in most cases, you worry about the state of your relationship due to the fact that you cannot reciprocate physical attention and affection to your partner.

People who suffer from Haphephobia might express different symptoms, unique to each individual. The severity of the symptoms will also depend on the individual, and the level of fear they are exposed to.

Many people who experience this phobia can usually tolerate touch but only when they initiate it, or allow their partner to initiate it. Over time, you can also gain enough trust in your partner to a point where you can overcome the phobic reactions when they touch you. Some people might completely be uncomfortable with any kind of touch. When it happens, you might shake, freeze up, feel the urge to run away, sweat, and in some cases, cry your eyes out.

Most of the time people who struggle with Haphephobia will keep their hands full so that they don't have to hug or shake hands with anyone. You might also avoid spending time with someone if you feel they are romantically interested in you.

Human touch in an intimate relationship is innate. Therefore, it is important that you learn how to overcome these challenges. Without this, you might struggle with isolation and even feel lonely while you are with your partner.

There are several therapeutic procedures that you can undertake to treat Haphephobia. With around 90% success in treatment, you will not have to suffer any longer. You can also talk to your partner so that they understand what you are afraid of, and you can even work on other ways of expressing affection when you are getting intimate.

Uneasiness When Discussing Sex

You are not alone. Many people struggle to talk about their sexual desires even to their partners. It is not just about the things that they love or want to be done to them, but this also concerns the things that they do not like. If you are unable to have such discussions, you prolong the inevitable. Your fears grow into obligations and over time, sex becomes a routine for you instead of something you enjoy with your partner.

Everyone has a unique reason why they are unable to talk about sex openly. For most people, it is about the way they were brought up. Some topics have always been taboo for as long as they have known them. Therefore, they find it awkward discussing or questioning something.

You need to learn how to communicate with your partner. Fortunately, communication does not necessarily have to involve spoken words. In many cases, words might even get in the way of the message if you cannot match your words to what your body wants to express. You can come up with a non-verbal method of alerting your partner whether they are doing something right. For those who struggle to conjure up the right words, how about a light murmur or whisper in your partner's ears when they do it right?

Concerning touch, you don't really have to tell your partner they are touching you inappropriately. A slight movement away from their touch can do the trick. Once you get used to such cues, you might find the courage to talk about the reasons why you move the way you do when your partner touches you in a certain way.

What you have to avoid, however, is suffering in silence. This never ends well. When you are quiet, your partner cannot know what is going on in your mind. They cannot tell whether they are doing it right or not. For most people who cannot be vocal about their needs, subtle gestures might do. However, if your partner is still not getting the hint, you can lightly hold their hand and show them how you want to be pleasured.

Remember that this is a learning process for both of you. Your partner might be used to doing things the way you don't like, so you both will have to learn to accommodate one another.

In case you make a subtle request for your partner to change something but they don't seem to be getting the hint, there is a possibility that they are fully immersed in the action, and are hardly in control of their cognitive function. This is true if they have been performing that particular action for quite a while. This does not mean that they are not paying attention to you, you simply need to nudge them gently and lovingly so they can snap back into their cognitive function and hear you out.

Chapter 6: Like Fine Wine, Better With Time

As we grow older, the desire to be close to the people we love increases. Whether it is our kids, siblings, parents or our partners, we crave that sense of belonging, the security that comes with being around people who mean everything to you. This desire can manifest in many ways. For some people, it is the desire to keep a healthy, satisfying, and active sex life. The problem is that our bodies change as we age, and this means that we might not be able to perform at the same level we used to a few years back. This also means that you must adapt your sexual activity to the demands of your body's physique, your health, and many other changes that take place.

Intimacy as you grow older can take place in many ways, whether you are enjoying it with your partner or on your own. You can express yourself in different types of stimulation or touch. Always remember that growing old is a part of life, and the changes that come with this growth will affect different aspects of your life. Sex is one of them.

Normal Changes You Might Experience

Normal changes are things that everyone expects to happen to their bodies as they grow old. You might have some problems here and there, but these are normal things. When you talk about them with your partner, you create an understanding that your bodies are changing, and you can adapt your sex life to accommodate the changes.

With time, your body experiences some physical changes in both men and women which might affect your ability to enjoy sex as you have always done, or even have it in the first place. Do not be surprised when some people decide to put off sex altogether because their bodies just cannot handle it.

For women, you will notice vaginal changes. As you grow older, your vagina might become narrow and shorter. As this happens, the vaginal walls might also become stiffer and thinner. As a result, some women do not have as much vaginal lubrication as they used to a few years back. Therefore, when engaging in sex with your partner, it might take you longer for natural vaginal lubrication.

As a result of such changes, you can expect some discomfort with vaginal penetration. This pain usually makes some women give up sex altogether. Instead of giving up sex, why not consider using water-based lube? Alternatively, you can also get yourself some lubricated condoms which will make the process more comfortable and enjoyable for you.

Other than women who might be put off by sex, there are instances where you might want to have more sex than before. This is particularly for women who are using hormone therapy to manage menopause symptoms. Hormone therapy can trigger changes in your body such that your desire to have sex is higher. Do not feel uncomfortable about this. Talk about it with your partner so that they can understand why all of a sudden, you are very horny most of the time.

When you grow old with your partner, it can be quite a buzzkill when one of you has an increased sex drive while the other is on a slump. If you don't discuss it openly, your partner might feel like they are not satisfying you, perhaps they are not good enough for you and so on. These are sentiments that could kill your intimacy. He needs assurance that his sex drive and yours are okay. Yours is just triggered by hormone therapy.

For men, one of the common challenges you experience as you grow older is erectile dysfunction. This refers to the inability to have or maintain an erection. If you suffer from erectile dysfunction, it might take you longer to get an erection. When you do, it might also not be as firm as it used to be a few years back.

After an orgasm, you will lose the erection faster and it might also take you longer before you get another erection. While erectile dysfunction is cause for alarm, every man gets it at some point. Therefore, if it happens to you from time to time, this should not be a problem. However, if you are experiencing these changes all the time, it is time you see a doctor.

For both men and women, these changes can affect your personality, especially when you don't understand them. The onset of these changes catches many people unaware, because it happens at a stage in your life where you are focusing on many other things like work, building your career, raising a family, working on investments and so forth. At this stage in your life, you get tired from all the things you do, and barely find time for intimacy. Most of the time all you need is to sleep. Therefore, when these changes happen, they creep in on you and by the time you realize what's happening, you have become so accustomed to dissatisfaction that giving up sex altogether comes easy for you.

Discuss these changes with your partner. Let them know what

you feel and how things that are happening in your lives are making you feel. Your doctor could actually recommend a few suggestions that might improve your sex life. More importantly, remember that this is a two-people thing.

Why Do These Problems Occur?

Impotence, sudden increase in sex drive, lack of enthusiasm about sex—all these are changes that we experience as we grow older. However, why do they happen? What happens in the body that gets us here?

The aging process is a culmination of many things that have happened in your life since you were born. Disabilities, illnesses, surgery, medicine, and everything else that might have happened to your body as you grow up is responsible for the way you age, and your ability to enjoy sex.

The following are some of the reasons why you might struggle to enjoy sex as you grow older:

- **Arthritis**

If you have arthritis, joint pains might make it very uncomfortable for you to have or enjoy sex. To counter this pain, your doctor might recommend joint replacement surgery, drugs, or exercise. Regarding your sex life, you might also want to consider a warm bath, rest, or change your sex schedule. As you can imagine, changing your sex schedule or even having sex on a schedule might sound too routine, so you have to discuss this with your partner so that they understand why you need to make these changes.

- **Chronic Pain**

As you grow older, chronic pain makes it difficult for you to enjoy intimate moments with your partner. The good thing about chronic pain is that it does not have to be the hill you die on. There are treatments for chronic pain that will help you overcome the strain. While chronic pain can be treated, take note that some of the medication might affect your sex drive. If you realize any unusual changes, discuss it with your doctor so they can recommend an alternative.

- **Diabetes**

For a lot of men, diabetes is one of the leading causes of erectile dysfunction. More often you can get help with early treatment. Instead of seeking help from a doctor, a lot of guys resort to enhancement pills like Viagra. Resist the urge to use such pills because you might get addicted to them, and in the process, risk heart problems.

There is not much information available concerning the effect of diabetes on older women and their sex drive. However, it is common for women with diabetes to experience yeast infections. The irritation and itching that comes with a yeast infection can make sex undesirable, painful, and uncomfortable. On the bright side though, there are treatments for yeast infections.

- **Dementia**

Dementia introduces unique challenges to the couple. In some cases, individuals who have dementia might experience an increase in the desire to have sex, or to be physically closer to someone. However, it might not be easy for them to tell what is an acceptable sexual approach. It gets worse when your partner has severe dementia because they might not be able to recognize you at all, while they still need to enjoy sex. As a result, it is possible they might innocently get sex from someone else. This can be a very painful and difficult scenario, so it is important to have someone around, such as an expert, to help.

- **Heart problems**

Heart problems affect your ability to have orgasms. The pulsation in the arteries might affect your blood vessels in such a way that blood cannot flow freely anymore. As a result, it might take you longer to get aroused. For men, however, you might struggle to get or maintain an erection.

If you or your partner have experienced a heart attack before, there is always that fear that engaging in sex might result in another attack. This makes many people shy away from sex altogether. Doctors advise that having sex is generally safe. Try, however, to follow the doctor's advise accordingly.

- **Incontinence**

Incontinence is common in men and women as they grow older. This is a condition where you lose control of your bladder, and leak urine from time to time. When you have sex, applying additional pressure on your stomache might make things worse. Therefore, if you struggle with incontinence as you grow older, consider trying different sex positions. Before you get intimate, you might also want to empty your bladder. On the bright side though, there are treatments for incontinence, so get in touch with your doctor.

- **Stroke**

If you have had a stroke before, it might affect your ability to have or enjoy sex. There are medical devices that you can use to assist, or change your preferred sex position. In fact, with the right kind of support, even individuals who have paralysis from their waist down can still enjoy pleasure and orgasms.

- **Depression**

One of the challenges of depression is that you lose interest in the things that you used to enjoy before. Sex and intimacy can easily become victims. Depression hits hard because in many cases, victims are unaware that they are depressed. It is important that you discuss with your doctor when you realize you are not as enthusiastic about some of the things you used to enjoy before. If you seek help as early as possible, you can treat depression and have a normal, happy, and satisfying sex life once again.

Readjusting The Sexual Dynamic In Your Relationship

It is a jungle out there. Growing up and growing older exposes us to a lot of things, many which we never thought we had to deal with, or at least not at the time when we had to. Our bodies go through a lot of physical changes over the years. Our hormonal levels also adjust at each stage of our lives, and the cumulative effect of these changes is that in some cases, we lose the desire to have or enjoy sex as we used to.

For many couples, it is difficult to come back from this slump, especially when you get comfortable in it. The challenge with this is that you never stay in the slump for long. In many cases, the slump only lasts until someone takes an interest in your life and gives you the kind of attention you needed, but never knew you had it in you to desire, and all hell breaks loose. This is how you end up in an affair in your 50's when you should be enjoying the company of your partner.

More often, sex is about perspectives. We all wish to maintain the same level of eroticism we had in our youth but the reality is that our lives cannot allow us to. When you grow older with someone, you learn to read and respond to their bodies over time. You learn to know what works for them and what doesn't. This makes a big difference and will help you know how to change your lifestyle and perceptions about sex as you grow older.

The fact is that for most people, the desire to have and enjoy sex fades away over time as they grow older. There are many reasons for this. We discussed quite a number of them in the section above. What you should realize is that these changes should not condemn you to an unhappy life without quality sex, or a life of obligatory sex without enjoying it.

Of course, at the onset of your relationship, the passion is incredible. You have sex almost all the time, you cannot keep your hands off each other even for a minute, and you are willing to try some amazing things and new techniques at the earliest opportunity. Sadly, physiological and psychological changes a few years down the line take a toll on you and you can no longer do the things you fancied, not for lack of trying though.

This slowdown happens in many relationships, and in some it

happens much sooner than expected. We live in a world that glorifies instant gratification and getting something new as soon as you get tired of the old one. This is not how healthy relationships work. You must put in the work. If your relationship is losing the spark, the following are some ideas that will help you rekindle the fire:

- **Play Together**

Just because you have been married a few years doesn't mean you should stop flirting. Surprise your partner with a sext from time to time. Share some raunchy jokes with them. The idea here is not necessarily to get them jumping into the sack with you, but to remind them how much fun it was to do those things together. This kind of play helps you oil the wheels of your relationship and before you know it, you will be having a lot of enjoyable and pleasurable sex.

- **Try New Things**

Forget about the bedroom. It gets boring and routine after a while. Forget about the backseat of your car too, unless you have not done that before. You might consider driving to a new place both of you have never been before and getting it on. As a couple, at times you need to try new experiences together to rekindle the fire.

The good thing about this is that it gives you so much to talk about, so much to reminisce about the good days when you were young and full of energy. The spontaneity of youthful dating can help you reignite the passion in your sex life.

- **Enjoy Your Partner's Schedule**

When was the last time you were interested in what your partner does for a living? If your partner is an artist, for example, when was the last time you snuck into their workshop to watch them paint? Better yet, why not have them create a work of art with you for a change? When someone is busy getting through their day, watching them with admiration makes them confident and proud. This also reminds them that in your eyes, they are desirable and lovable.

- **A Walk Down Memory Lane**

It might not be possible for you to revisit some of the places you went on dates in the past, but you can try with those you can. Try to relive that experience where necessary. Order your meal at a restaurant and sit in the same spot you sat during your first date. Order the same meal you had on that day.

Don't end it there. When you get home, remind one another about the things you used to enjoy doing to each other in bed. Talk about the way you enjoyed each other's company, the tricks your partner did that made you aroused and so on. This is not just about the history of your lives, it will also help you create an element of mystery over the coming weeks.

- **Adore Each Other**

You tell everyone you love and cherish your partner; everyone, that is, but them. As we grow into relationships, in many cases the fire fizzles out for different reasons. One of the things we gradually forget to do is to compliment our partner, even for no reason. How many times have you stopped your partner right before they head out the door, just to admire and gaze at them, and remind them that they are amazing? How often do you tell your partner that you adore them and appreciate everything you have been through together, and the awesomeness that they bring into your life?

The beauty of such compliments is that they often come with an unwritten rule of reciprocity. Your partner will feel the need to reciprocate the sentiments. If they have not been paying attention, they will be keener on the things you do so that they can find something to compliment you about. The desire that was once lacking in your relationship soon finds a way back gradually, and this will also extend into your sexual life.

- **Proactiveness**

You must learn how to be proactive and forthcoming about certain things in your relationship. This is a good way to reignite the fire and bring back the desire. There are many things that you can try as couple activities, like reading an adult novel out loud, couples' massage or a bath.

You can also change the way you do things in the house. Say you undress and brush your teeth before going to bed. Why not intercept your partner before they do, and make out with them before they get into the routine? Routine can be boring, but you can also tweak things a bit and get your partner wondering where the animal in you came from.

You might not know it yet, but even subtle changes will always make sex feel different. The idea here is to come up with a scenario where you cannot predict what your partner will do next, and the anticipation excites you.

Chapter 7: The Plan of Attack

Sex is an intimate act that we share for different reasons. While it is possible to enjoy sex with someone other than your partner, the concept of sex espoused in this book is about sex between intimate partners. This is sex between individuals who hold one another in high regard, who value and appreciate one another.

Throughout this book we have discussed several concepts about sex, from the history through different civilizations to how you can get intimate with your partner. One of the challenges that most people have is that we cannot admit when we fall short, especially when it comes to sex. No one wants to feel or be seen as inadequate. With such thoughts, we hold back and in many cases, struggle to talk about important things in our sex lives.

A resounding message in this book is the need for communication. Many couples do not communicate, and those who do, do not do it effectively. Communication is just about as intimate as sex with your partner. There is a way you can talk to your partner that makes them feel comfortable and confident, such that they can open up and tell you something that worries them, especially about your sex life. There is also a way you can talk to your partner that makes them feel awkward, terrible, and disappointed they even tried opening up to you in the first place.

There are many ways we can explore the depths of our sexuality. You can do it alone, or with your partner. The important lesson here is that many of us barely know what our bodies are about, or why we think and do things the way we do them when it comes to sex. This is another aspect of communication that we need to emphasize. Communication is not just about talking to your partner about things that work for you or how, you also need to show them.

We learn that many people are unaware of what their bodies are about, regarding their sexual organs. This is a problem because for the most part, if you cannot understand what happens in your body, it is not easy for someone else to get it right. This problem comes from many possible sources, with the biggest culprit being our upbringing. We have a lot of people who grow up in a conservative environment where topics such as sex and sexuality are taboo subjects. This hinders their sexual education, and they either grow up ignorant or misinformed about sex and sexuality.

As we grow up, the inhibitions we harbor in our lives since childhood or adolescence about sex manifest in our sex lives, too. We find it difficult to open up and discuss or admit some shortcomings because we were not brought up to talk about such things. This is where many relationships struggle. The course of this book is to help you overcome the many challenges you have experienced in life about sex, and to give you a new lease on life. You are not too old to have and enjoy good sex. Your relationship is not too far gone either. You can turn things around, and with this book, you will not only know how, but also how to sustain the changes.

Fundamentals of Sex and Sexuality

Over the course of this book, we realized that many of the sexual challenges we experience are as a result of misunderstandings. Misunderstandings could manifest in the form of assumptions, miscommunication, and many other ways. As long as there is no clear message between partners, it becomes a problem to understand what each one wants.

Sexual desire is normal, and even when faced with different physical and emotional changes in life, our desire to have an intimate encounter with our partner does not go away. Many people do not get to enjoy this because they don't know how to talk about what they want.

You have to embrace your sexuality, love your body, and learn to understand it. There is a lot you can learn about your body when you take the time and listen to it. You have so much to learn that will help you be more enlightened and appreciate yourself. Most of the struggles we experience with sex happen because many people do not feel they deserve to feel sexually desirable. Such are the kind of thoughts that we should eliminate altogether.

Sex is a beautiful act that brings you closer to your loved one, and promotes intimacy in your relationship. Unfortunately, many people cannot tell the difference between intimacy and sex. These are two different concepts, and your ability to tell them apart gets you closer to a level of sexual intelligence that many people crave but cannot achieve.

What Should I Do?

The first thing you have to do is realize that sex is about understanding. You can't just rush it when you are trying to get intimate with your partner. The kind of understanding you need to enjoy sex with your partner means that you listen, not just to what you talk about, but more importantly, listen to their body. This is not an easy thing to do, especially if you barely listen to your body in the first place.

You need to connect with your partner at a different level than you connect with everyone else. This is part of forming a love language that only the two of you understand. This connection is unique, such that no one but the two of you can understand it. If you try this connection with someone else, it should feel off and awkward.

While you might learn how to read the mood and understand what your partner wants, one of the important lessons you should take from this book is the need to be confident in yourself. Your desires are valid, and you should be heard. You have to make your intentions known. A bit of guesswork in sex is good, especially when you are being playful, but in many cases, your intentions should be explicit.

When you need attention, make your partner know you need their attention. You can be subtle or direct about it, but do it in a way that does not make them feel uncomfortable. At the same time, as you crave attention, you must also learn to express the same to your partner. This is a give and take situation, and you should give as much as you are willing to receive. In the long run, this helps you develop a mutual respect for each other and you see one another as equal partners in the relationship.

There will be times when you do not feel like having sex. This is normal. Every relationship goes through such moments. However, you should not make it your personal torture chamber. Emotional and physical challenges can make you lose interest in sex. Instead of shutting your partner out, make an effort and talk to them about your reasons for losing interest. During such trying moments, it is important to understand the underlying reasons before you address the issue at hand.

Ultimate Sexual Intelligence

When it comes to sexual intelligence, there is so much that you will learn when you read this book. Sexual intelligence is about combining your knowledge of sexual matters, a healthy emotional state and understanding of your body and what it needs. You often wonder what makes some people better at sex than others, and it probably has nothing to do with their physique, though that might also help to some extent. It is primarily about getting the three facets of sexual intelligence aligned.

Being knowledgeable about sex makes a big difference in your life. There is so much we assume about sex and the effect on our sexual lives is profound. You have to let go of your inhibitions or anything else that you might have learned about sex from your childhood that makes you think differently. Confront the things that you believe are taboos and approach sex with an open mind. You will realize there is so much you can enjoy when you go through life this way.

Emotional scars can also hold you back and prevent you from enjoying a healthy sexual life. Many of these scars can be overcome. You just need to speak to your therapist, or open up and talk about them with your partner. In the case of childhood traumas, you will need special help from an expert. When you overcome these challenges, you can then unlock the heights of your sexuality that will enable you to have a lot of fun with your partner.

Finally, learn to appreciate one another in your body as you are. Forget about everything society has taught you about what a sexy body looks like. Your partner is the best version of themselves, and you should encourage them to see themselves that way if they are ever having doubts. Embrace them as they are, embrace yourself, and love that body because it is a sexual and attractive body, and your partner loves it.

Conclusion

Sex has always been a controversial topic. A lot of people cannot speak openly about it for different reasons. Many of us have inhibitions that prevent us from enjoying sex with our loved ones. There are many shared views about sex and sexuality that go a long way in influencing our perceptions, our lives, and our happiness. Many people are in relationships that feel empty because they cannot openly discuss sex. This is one of the reasons why a lot of relationships are failing today.

In this book, we have discussed several issues regarding sex that many people can relate to. These are things that happen on a daily basis, struggles that you are all too familiar with already. The approach we used in this book is to address many of the problems we have about sex and sexuality from a fundamental perspective. More often, we try to deal with symptoms of the problems we are facing instead of tackling the problem itself. This is where a lot of people go wrong.

One thing about our society that stands out is the way we are open to trying new things, new experiences and learning. This is a good thing, given that many people really do need to learn about sex afresh. Most of the information we have about sex comes from unworthy sources, lessons from our peers that were often influenced by the wrong ideas. Sex as we know it today might seem enlightened, but we are not the first generation to embrace it. To give you a glimpse of the history of sex, we discussed sex through different cultures and civilizations. You might also learn more about sex in your private studies especially if you are into anthropology.

Over the years, perceptions about sex have changed. Traditional societies had a narrow view of sex, where it was more of an obligation especially for women. Many such societies only focused on sex as a means of reproduction. The problem with this is that it took away the pleasure of sex, especially for the woman.

Sex is a beautiful act that should be shared and enjoyed by willing and consenting partners. Without this, it lacks respect and is no more than a means to an end, a power struggle. Today we live in an enlightened and liberated society where people view sex differently. We have learned through different sources, media, and other literature about the beauty of sex. Our generation is one that we can admit is experiencing the height of sexual revolution. People are more welcoming, embracing different cultures and sexual orientations. There are so many sexual orientations in the world at the moment, all who try to coexist peacefully with each other.

Most of the misconceptions about sex come from the fact that we do not really know what we want from sex. This is one of the honest conversations we should have with ourselves. While addressing this issue, we explained some of the common reasons why people pursue sex the way they do. However, sex is not just about the pursuit. There is more to it beyond the physical aspect. In this regard, we introduced the psychology of sex, to understand the real reasons why men and women regard each other the way they do when it comes to sex. While most of our physical reasons for having sex are similar, to a large extent our emotional and psychological needs are not wired the same. Most women seek something deeper from a sexual partner. They seek intimacy, love, comfort and security. For men, on the other hand, sex could easily be physical with no emotional attachments whatsoever. This is why most of the time men and women have differing views about each other.

Our societies and communities are part of the environment where we are brought up. Such environments have a profound effect on our expectations about sex. They influence our minds, thoughts, and views of sex. If you are honest, you will realize that almost everything you know or believe about sex and sexual relations is in some way influenced by the society you grew up in.

The thing about such upbringing is that there are some sexual acts and behaviors that are considered taboos. A taboo generally is something that a select community views as deviant behavior. Irrespective of what engaging in the act means to you personally, members of your community will see you as an outcast if they know you engage in it.

Learning from these taboos, our communities condition us from a young age into a certain thought pattern about sexual norms. There are things that are expected of you if you engage in sex with your partner, and many others that are considered abhorrable acts. How society conditions you influences your perspective of sex even when you are with your partner. You might even struggle to enjoy some things because you were brought up to believe they are terrible.

All the taboos you learn about sex are not necessarily true. In fact, today a lot of people are more open to trying the things that are considered taboo, and in the process, many have come to realize that it is all a matter of perception. What you do behind closed doors with your partner should not concern anyone other than yourselves, especially since it delivers the pleasure that strengthens your bond together.

Enjoying sex is one thing, but enjoying sex with your partner requires a level of sexual intelligence that many people lack. Sex is about sharing yourself, your intimate moments with someone special. This, however, is not always the case. There are many people who engage in meaningless sex for the sole purpose of satisfying their carnal needs. This is also okay as long as you know what you are after.

In this book, our discussions about sex concern so much more than the one night stand. Our discussions are about healthy sexual intimacy between people who have a lot more in common than a pint at the bar. Our discussions are about two lovers who have built a life together, and need to rekindle or maintain that spark in their lives. Sexual intelligence is an elaborate approach to sex that requires three things; knowledge about sex and sexual intimacy, your awareness of your emotional health and more importantly, a good understanding of your body and the changes that it goes through over time.

The human body is a work of art, but a complicated one. As we grow older, the body goes through a series of changes that eventually affect all aspects of our lives. One of the areas where these changes are profound is our sexual lives. Your knowledge and awareness of your sexual ability will go a long way in helping you learn the important steps you need to take in life to accommodate these changes. Remember that you are not growing old alone. Your partner is growing old, too. Therefore, these are discussions you should have together, considering that they feel the effects of the changes your body goes through, and how it affects your sexual life.

When it comes to matters sexual, we all tend to believe ourselves the best lovers our partners will come across.

However, this is not always the case. You must try and learn how to involve your brain and emotional IQ in sexual matters. The brain and your body must align for you to get any chance at enjoying sexual wholesomeness. This is important because you will learn about the things that turn you on, the things that make you uncomfortable, and how these affect your sexual life.

We are often inhibited in our sexual abilities by a lot of the things that we learn. Sexual inhibition makes it difficult for many people to express themselves freely. There are many times when instead of expressing your desires, you are afraid and hold back because of emotional scars, insecurities about your body, discomfort when you are around other people, or perhaps lack of confidence about yourself. These are things you should openly discuss with your partner so that they can help you get through it.

Finally, our bodies go through a lot of changes, which affect our sexual desires and drive. There are physical and emotional changes that we experience which affect our perception of sex and sexuality. These also make you feel less desirable or lose confidence and interest in sex. Since these changes are inevitable, worrying about them will only make things worse and prevent you from enjoying sex. Instead, you can work your way through it by readjusting your perspective, and more importantly, learning how to accept yourself the way you are.

References

Arneth, B. M. (2009). Sexual selection and intelligence: Does sexual reproduction drive the evolution of intelligence? Bioscience Hypotheses, 2(4).

Donohue, W. (2018). The Catholic Church and Sexual Abuse. In I. Horowitz, Culture & Civilization: Volume Four: Religion in the Shadows of Modernity (pp. 13–34). Routledge.

Moslener, S. (2015). Sexual Purity and Civilization Work in the 19th Century. In S. Moslener, Virgin Nation: Sexual Purity and American Adolescence (pp. 16–47). Oxford University Press.

Nijman, H., Merckelbach, H., & Cima, M. (2009). Performance intelligence, sexual offending and psychopathy. Journal of Sexual Aggression, 15(3), 319–330.

O'Brien, C. C. (2003). Race-ing Toward Civilization: Sexual Slavery and Nativism in the Novels of Pauline Elizabeth Hopkins and Alice Wellington Rollins. Legacy, 20(1).

Rahman, Q., Bhanot, S., Emrith-Small, H., Ghafoor, S., & Roberts, S. (2012). Gender nonconformity, intelligence, and sexual orientation. Archives of Sexual Behavior, 41(3), 623–630.

Schultz, G. (2012). Transnationalism and sexual identity in literature: from the French canon to US pulp fiction. Contemporary French Civilization, 37(2–3).

Willi, J., & Burri, A. (2015). Emotional Intelligence and Sexual Functioning in a Sample of Swiss Men and Women. The Journal of Sexual Medicine, 12(10), 2051–2060.

Made in the USA
Coppell, TX
17 August 2022